JAMES ACASTER'S GUIDE TO QUITTING SOCIAL MEDIA

By James Acaster and available from Headline

James Acaster's Classic Scrapes
Perfect Sound Whatever

JAMES ACASTER'S GUIDE TO QUITTING SOCIAL MEDIA

Being the best YOU you can be and saving yourself from loneliness

Vol. 1

HEADLINE

First published in 2022 by
HEADLINE PUBLISHING GROUP

1

Cataloguing in Publication Data is available from the British Library

Hardback ISBN 978 1 4722 8856 1

Typeset in Monotype Sabon by CC Book Production
Printed and bound in Great Britain by Clays Ltd, Elcograf S.p.A.

MIX
Paper from
responsible sources
FSC® C104740

Headline's policy is to use papers that are natural, renewable and recyclable
products and made from wood grown in well-managed forests and other
controlled sources. The logging and manufacturing processes are expected
to conform t   origin.

For the Tangfastic Crew, too many to name x

Introduction

Hello, Social Media Addict and welcome to the greatest book you will ever own.

Within these pages you will find the secrets to living free of the Internet, free of Sadness, and free of Self-Help Books (eventually). My name is James Acaster, I'm a phenomenal teacher, a terrific guru, a constant inspiration to many, and I'm about to take your poxy reality and flip it on its head till the wheels fall off.

I used to be like you: a saddo, hopelessly chasing validation from strangers online, eyes glued to my phone screen like two spherical fridge magnets, believing that the answer to all of my worries would miraculously pop up on my timeline and save my tattered soul. But those days are over. I'm now one of the best people in the world and it's all because I don't have any social media presence. I once was lost, yes, but now I'm found. I once was blind, sure, but now I see. I once was on the internet but now I'm off the internet.

But take heed, my little lost lamb babies, I can only provide you with the essential tools here – YOU'RE the one who has to pick them up and chisel out an existence for yourself. YOU'RE the one who has to quit social media for good and start anew. YOU'RE the one who has to deal with being a failure if this book doesn't 'work'. Not me. The clue's in the name – it's *self*-help not *James*-help. I'm the one *telling* you to help yourself – that is all. Which means I'm also the person who can take all the credit if you actually succeed. So everybody wins.

For best results, I recommend reading this entire book in one sitting without taking any breaks. You can divide it up into smaller chunks and read it over an extended period of time if that's 'easier' for you, but don't blame me if you're still hooked on social media by page 36,576. Instead, take a long hard look in the mirror, or the nearest reflective surface, and blame yourself (out loud if possible and using your full name). I have created this book in order to save you from your own idiocy. It's intended to serve as, in the words of Dave Gahan, your own personal Jesus. And, just like Jesus, it can only work its magic if you accept it into your heart and denounce all that came before it. Otherwise you will spend eternity in Hell. That means giving all computers the old middle finger salute just like the disciples did to the Devil.

So close your eyes, take a deep breath, and start reading (after opening your eyes again). Your new life begins now.

Thank you*,

James Acaster

---

* Is what you'll be saying to me when you finish this book.

The Beginning

Outside of Tom, I was the first person to join MySpace. The year was 2003, Tom had built and launched the site himself and now he just needed to fill it. Fill it with what? Fill it with friends: enough like-minded individuals to start a digital revolution. An online community passionate about building a better tomorrow, each with their own awe-inspiring profile detailing what made their visionary brains tick. But no one showed up. No one, that is, until a happy-go-lucky, eighteen-year-old swell by the name of James Acaster stumbled upon the site completely by accident.

The site I'd intended to visit was the ever-reliable MySpade.com, for reasons I'm sure you can figure out on your own. I expected to be greeted by a looped animation of a rosy-cheeked gardener digging a brilliant hole but, thanks to some wonky-fingered typing, found myself staring at an unfamiliar homepage featuring two bits of 'news'.

News item number one stated that the site, named MySpace, had been officially launched. I glanced at the top of the screen and took in the (now iconic) MySpace logo. This was not MySpade.com. I glanced down at my keyboard and noted that the D key was one row up and diagonally to the left of the C key. Could've happened to anyone.

News item number two announced that a person named Tom had created their 'MySpace profile'. I was coloured a distinct shade of curious so decided to put 'Project Moat' on hold and investigate further. I clicked on the story regarding this Tom character, the story took me to his profile page and my life changed forever.

Tom

A man sat at his computer with his back to me, looking over his shoulder, smiling like an old and faithful chum. This was Tom. He looked like a good guy, the sort of friend who behaves decently 97 per cent of the time but occasionally lets himself down by making a poorly judged joke about your mum. 'Who's this?' I thought to myself, then immediately received the answer by reading the rest of his MySpace profile. What an experience. As the second person on MySpace, I became the first person to read someone else's social media profile. In doing so, I also became the first person to feel jealous of a total stranger for no good reason. This Tom fella had a whole page of the internet devoted to him like he was a bona fide celebrity – like a Brad Pitt or Andi Peters figure. Tom was a star and I was a piece-a-shit nobody who could fall off the face of the Earth and no one would even notice because I had zero internet presence due to being a loser who stinks. Within seconds I'd made up my mind – I needed MySpace pronto. I needed MySpace more than I had ever needed anything, more than I needed a spade even. And I badly needed a spade, otherwise I'd recently got a drawbridge fitted for nothing. I joined MySpace right there and then and my life changed forever (again).

James

Within a matter of minutes, it was official: I, James William Jericho Acaster, would forever be known as the second person to set up their MySpace profile page. I'd filled out every incredible detail about myself:

Favourite film – *March of the Penguins 2: Still Marchin'*
Favourite music – MOTP2:SM OST
Hobbies – castle construction (amateur)

For the first time ever, I was officially a Somebody. My days of being a Nobody were over. My days of being just Anybody were a thing of the past. My days of being a Busybody . . . well, I won't lie, they're still going strong. I love the busybody life. So sue me.

As if to affirm my new Somebody status, immediately after launching my profile I became the *first person ever* to receive a MySpace friend request – and when I saw who the request was from, I couldn't believe my fucking eyes. It was from Tom. Not Tom Cruise nor Tom Allen, not Little Tommy Tomkins nor Dr Tomatoes Thompson. It was Tom-the-man-who-owned-MySpace-Tom, the Tom in charge, the Big Tom (the person, not the popular brand of tomato juice, although that still would've been cool). I felt special and important – my MySpace profile must've been pretty spectacular if the top brass were already sniffing round my door. I'd been on the site for a matter of seconds and the inner circle wanted to be my *friend*. They wanted us to go to each other's houses for tea. They wanted to throw a frisbee back and forth and slag off other friends behind their backs. I stared at his friend request, trying to get a feel for the chap. Even back then, Tom's photo felt iconic – his eyes the dictionary definition of moist as he flashed me two rows of soon-to-be-trademark pearly-whites. I immediately saw myself in him. Mainly because he was sitting at his computer and I was currently sitting at my computer also. The photo told me he was affable (friendly smile) yet devoted to his work (sat at his computer). The kind of guy who wouldn't think twice about making a batch of spaghetti bolognese for his housemates but also made no apologies for needing time alone to meet his deadlines, presumably taking his own bowl of bolognese into his room while he worked, resulting in a keyboard dotted with tiny orange sauce stains.

'The sauce gives the keyboard character!' Tom would say as he laughed off any criticism from his bozo housemates who were giving him shit about his keyboard despite the fact he'd just kindly made them dinner. What a gent. As I gazed in awe, I wondered what Tom made of *my* profile picture – a shot of me getting blasted in the face by a hand dryer in the Burger King toilets. There was only one way to find out. I clicked on the only word that made sense – 'accept' – and, for the third time that day, my life changed forever.

Tom & James

For six wonderful months everything was perfect. MySpace belonged to Tom and me alone. We were able to hang out and shoot the shit 24/7. And when I say 24/7 I mean *literally* 24/7. I never left my computer and no longer needed sleep because friendship gave me all the energy I needed – like a hypodermic needle loaded with Red Bull straight to my heart, eyeballs and butt. Also, when I say 'shoot the shit' I mean we talked to each other, that's all I mean. Some things in this book I mean literally (e.g. '24/7'), others I don't (e.g. 'shoot the shit'). I'm going to need you to tell the difference by yourselves, otherwise most of this will be me explaining what is and isn't meant literally and that's not a book – it's most arguments on Twitter (*explosion noise*). With that in mind, let's see how you do with this next literal *or non-literal* sentence: Tom and I were the Adam and Eve of social media. We had the run of the garden and there wasn't a single low-down dirty conniving serpent in sight – just me and Tom Space. Oh yeah, Tom's surname is Space. Most people don't know that because they never got as close to him as I did. It's no big deal, he just told me his surname one day because he trusts me and thinks I'm rad. The man's surname is Space. Mr Thomas Space. Let's move on.

It was a true honour to share MySpace exclusively with its Creator. 'Creator' may seem like an intimidating title but there was no getting around it: Tom was essentially the God of this particular Garden of Eden. So when I said it was like we were Adam and Eve earlier, I was a little bit off. We were like God and Adam. Like if God had created Adam and then, because he thought Adam was a supremely rad guy, decided to just chill with Adam by himself instead of creating Eve. In fact, because Adam was so cool, God probably wouldn't create any other humans. Meaning that when God eventually wrote the Bible, the only person around to read it would be Adam, who'd just get handed a book written by his best friend about how awesome their friendship was. *That's* what me and Tom were like.

I was on MySpace so much that I didn't engage with anyone else, on- or offline. As far as the rest of the world was concerned,

I'd gone AWOL (Absent While On Line) and people were genu-inely worried about me. My boring family and dull-ass friends couldn't understand why I'd rather spend every waking hour staring at a magical computer screen than have excruciating real-life interactions with them. But, hey, of course they didn't understand – they'd never met Tom Space. They had no idea what MySpace felt like, only *their* space.

Well. All of that was about to change. Forever.

Ernie Freedman

I remember the first day a brand-new user showed up. Back then, I would always begin each morning by reading every single page on the MySpace website. All four of them. The homepage, Tom's page, my page and, if I was feeling sentimental, the T's and C's. One morning, while doing my rounds, I encountered an unexpected addition to the family: a brand-new profile for someone who was neither me nor Tom (nor, I would later discover, a decent human being). The profile belonged to a fella by the name of Ernie Freedman (an arsehole but, again, I didn't know that yet), a 49-year-old travelling salesman from Idaho whose profile picture consisted of him in a plaid shirt, sleeves rolled up, mugging at the camera and lightly sweating as he tucked into a steak the size of a child's surfboard (upon reflection, red flags everywhere).

Tom was giddier than I'd ever seen him.

'Shall we send friend requests, JPeg? I will if you will!'

I didn't see why not. I remembered how special I'd felt when I received my very first friend request so I could only imagine how Ernie Freedman would feel when *the* God and *the* Adam of MySpace asked to be his friend! This must've been how Eve felt when she sprang to life from an enchanted rib and was greeted by *the* Tom and *the* James Acaster of the Bible. This double act was about to become a terrific trio and as a big fan of Hanson, *The Lord of the Rings* and the amount of times Lionel Richie's wife was a lady, I could barely contain myself. But then something unsettling happened. Something that still turns my stomach to this very day. Ernie Freedman accepted Tom's friend request – *totally cool, glad he did* – but *not* mine. Oh. Dear.

I tried not to take the ghosting personally but that's hard to do when it's objectively personal. Just to recap, there were only three of us on the site and this new guy waltzes in like a big stinking turd in a bow tie, only wanting to be friends with *one* of the other *two* people?! What's the point of joining a social networking site if you're only going to befriend *one* person?!

Yes, I myself had only befriended one person when I joined MySpace but I didn't have a choice. Back then, there was only one other person on the site so by befriending him, I befriended *everyone* on MySpace and no one else in the history of the internet can claim to have ever been friends with *everyone* on MySpace so, guess what – that makes me the most popular person ever. AND YET, even though I was *the most popular person ever*, one question remained – WHY DIDN'T ERNIE FREEDMAN WANT TO BE MY FRIEND?! It's not like he could've been put off by my profile picture. I'd recently adopted the white T-shirt and blue jeans look (AKA 'The Tom'), binned the Burger King photo and recreated Tom's profile pic, using it as my own. The ultimate act of friendship. If he liked Tom Space, he had to like me too! I kept refreshing my page to see if Ernie Freedman had come to his senses and accepted my goddamn fucking friend request but there was nothing. In the days that followed, Tom and Freedman hit it off big time. They read each other's MySpace blogs *the moment they got posted* – like they were the new Harry Potter book or some shit. They wrote on each other's walls like they were Banksy and another graffiti artist beside Banksy. Meanwhile, I was receiving half the Tom-Time I used to get because he'd had his head turned by Ernie fucking Freedman. It was like if God created Adam and then God, of all people, befriended the serpent and ate the apple himself even though the serpent lacked the common decency to offer Adam an apple also. And then things got a whole lot worse.

After Ernie had kicked the door in with his filthy stinking crud-boots, the users arrived in droves. Unlike me, Loose-Lipped Ernie had recommended the site to every single one of his awful family and gormless friends. Ernie's idiot mates predictably told even more of their insufferable pals about MySpace, who told even more bozos and before I knew it, the place was overrun with dum-dums. I know inviting your mates sounds like the obvious thing to do but I never saw the point of inviting people I already knew onto the site. I frequently saw and spoke to them in my day-to-day life so why would I want to speak to them online also? On MySpace I could speak to anyone in the entire world, from any continent, any country, any city, so why would I choose to speak to Andy who lived next door to me and who I already saw whenever I took the bins out? If I'd blabbed to everyone about MySpace from the word go, I never would've had six months of hanging out with Tom one-on-one – something I'd clearly never get to do again thanks to a steak-chomping, travelling salesdick and his bozo cohorts. Speaking of Tom – that needy weasel sent friend requests to every single boring numbskull who joined MySpace and they *all* accepted his friendship without hesitation. Before long, I was lucky if I got a solitary 'hello' from Tom, even though I was sending him cheery hellos every minute, on the minute. That guy had spread himself thinner than Chalamet on a Master Cleanse, and, if I'm honest, I was starting to feel like a Nobody again. I tried to play hard to get by changing my 'top friends' settings, reducing the list from eight to four, like it was some exclusive club that only accepted the crème de la crème. But alas, no one noticed I'd done this, due to me only having four MySpace friends to begin with. OK, since you're asking: Tom Space, a fake Gary Neville account and my parents. My parents had found out about MySpace from their friends Debbie and Lionel. I didn't want to accept their friend requests but while they didn't directly threaten to cut me out of their wills should I reject them, it was heavily implied.

The dictionary defines a friend as 'a person with whom one has a bond of mutual affection, typically one devoid of sexual or familial relations' but now the word 'friend' had morphed into a hollow collection of letters that anyone could use to describe whatever they wanted e.g. a ball, a kitchen sink or an idiot who rolls his sleeves up to eat a steak. MySpace was making me miserable but I was still hooked. I wanted to leave but couldn't bear the thought of everyone having fun without me. So I stuck around and became more bitter and resentful by the day. Like goddamn Gollum. I was Gollum, Tom was The Precious, Ernie Freedman was an ugly orc with no brain and I had to figure out a way to leave The Shire. Fortunately, this problem was soon solved for me thanks to the invention of Facebook (AKA the boiling volcanoes of Mordor).

Facebook to the Rescue

It was 2006 and word was spreading about a new social media site that featured a different colour scheme to MySpace (blue with some white as opposed to white with some blue). Facebook didn't have any bands on there (meaning they were offering *less* than MySpace) but, besides that, it was exactly the same. I still don't fully understand why Facebook defeated MySpace so easily. When someone went on your MySpace page, your favourite song would automatically start playing. When someone went on your Facebook page, they were met with silence. So in the battle of music versus silence, the world chose silence. I believe the steady collapse of the music industry over the years that followed speaks for itself. Maybe Facebook simply seemed cooler, more stylish, more grown up than MySpace due to being less fun – who knows. Whatever the reason, there was a new God in Computer Town. His name was Zuckerberg and he was so cool he didn't ask to be friends with any of us – he just spied on us and sold our personal information to huge corporations until a guy who looked like a synth player ratted him out to the feds.

But back to 2006. I remember logging on to MySpace one morning and beginning my standard routine of reading every single page on the site. By this point, reading every single

MySpace page would literally take me all day. I'd wake up, look at every single page on MySpace, sleep for ten minutes then rise with the sun and do it all again. But this particular morning was different. I sat, aghast, and watched as profile page after profile page vanished before my very eyes. Users were jumping ship by the shedload, as if they'd only just noticed the ship was full of stinking, flea-ridden rats. And yes, I am calling all of the users rats. And yes, I'm also saying everyone was trying to get away from said rats. BUT the image of loads of rats jumping ship to get away from each other only to fill a different ship with the very same rats sums the situation up perfectly.

As I watched the masses flee, the idea of leaving MySpace didn't feel so scary any more. Clearly I would be missing out on fuck all. So I made the bold and brave decision to go ahead and quit the site for good. I sanitised my typing fingers and began to delete my profile. But before I could click the final 'Eliminate' button, I got a notification. A private message from Tom himself.

'Friends don't treat friends like this, JPeg, or should I say, J-udas!'

He'd altered his profile pic. He was still sitting at his computer, looking over his shoulder, only now he was in floods of ugly tears with drool and snot streaming from his contorted mug. He was playing hardball and I had a decision to make.

I know I shouldn't have but I did feel weirdly guilty. Back when I'd joined MySpace, I made a promise: 'to stand by my MySpace friends and support them to the very end, til death do us part', as it was written in the T's and C's (which I had read many, many times over). My parents and the fake Gary Neville account had long flown the coop but Tom was staying true. He'd honoured the sacred T's and C's and was pleading with me to do the same. Sure, he was doing it in a psychotic fashion but I couldn't argue with the logic – if I left MySpace, I was officially a BFF (a bad fucking friend).

Trapped

I didn't leave MySpace until the year 2020 and let me tell you, those fourteen years were the weirdest of my life. By the end of 2006, there were only six of us left: myself, my 'friend' Tom who owned MySpace, American comedian Dane Cook, Ernie fucking Freedman, indie rock band Arctic Monkeys and, confusingly, another guy named Tom. Original MySpace Tom was essentially holding the rest of us captive. We all felt like we owed him something and couldn't leave for fear of breaking his heart. Every single day was like being at a dictator's birthday party. We all had to pretend we loved MySpace: posting positive messages on each other's walls, changing our profile pictures to increasingly happier photos. I lost count of the amount of times I 'liked' something when in actual fact I disliked it. All the while knowing that if our enthusiasm dwindled, all hell would break loose. I sneakily joined other social media sites in the meantime but Tom would always follow me onto them (under the alias Thom) and comment on my posts with 'J-udas', 'T-raitor' or 'B-ad friend'. I don't know if he'd forgotten that he'd only added a hyphen to Judas in order to emphasise the J and make it sound more like my original nickname JPeg, but this was how he insulted me now. N-othing he did made sense. The final straw was when I woke up one morning to discover Tom had written a bunch of mad shit on my wall. Not my MySpace wall – my actual bedroom walls. He had snuck into my bedroom overnight and written messages everywhere. Stuff like, 'Never leave', 'Friends 'til Death' and, 'Hey man, I know you're thinking about leaving MySpace but if you could not then that'd be just dandy'. I knew it was Tom because of the formatting: he wrote his name first in blue, then the post in black, and finally, in grey, how long ago the post had been made. When I woke up it said 'five hours ago' and, according to an eyewitness who saw Tom clamber through my bedroom window, those timings were accurate. I still don't know how he did this.

Between his antics on MySpace and the recent home invasion, I couldn't get away from this guy and was left with only one choice. It was with a heavy heart that I took out a restraining order on my friend Tom. As in a real-life restraining order, I didn't just block him online. I still feel guilty from time to time but when a friend becomes a stalker, you have to take action, even when that friend is Tom (Original MySpace Tom, not the other Tom on MySpace, who is actually a really sound guy). As soon as the restraining order was activated, I deleted my MySpace account, spat on my computer screen and was finally free.

Post Space

As far as I know, the rest of the gang are still trapped there. Arctic Monkeys are forced to upload a new track every week, most of which feature lyrics about how handsome Tom Space is. Dane Cook is expected to post a funny comedy video every hour on the hour, usually an observational routine about having to endlessly listen to Arctic Monkeys. From what I gather, Ernie

Freedman still likes it there and hasn't even noticed everyone else has left (because he's a loser and his brain is made of dogshit). Even though I had to take out a restraining order on him, I do hope my friend Tom is OK (again, I'm talking about Tom *Space* here but I also hope the other Tom is OK. He was honestly so sound). Tom was a good friend once and I know, deep down, he just felt scared that everyone was abandoning him and buddying up elsewhere. In truth, I still carry some sadness with me and wish things could've been resolved in a more loving and respectful manner. That being said, he once showed up to a playpark I was at with my nephews and I tasered him. So, I also don't feel bad at all.

It's hard to describe the relief I felt when leaving MySpace. It was like I'd broken out of prison after a lifetime of solitary confinement and I could finally kiss my wife again. Deleting MySpace changed how I felt about the other social media sites I belonged to. They were fun, sure, but not as fun as quitting MySpace had been. Quitting MySpace made me feel strong and powerful for the first time in almost two decades. I'd been chained to this website as if my very sanity depended on it when in fact the opposite was true. Now I'd broken free and reclaimed control of my own narrative, I was alive again. Then a thought occurred to me: *I could quit them all.* I could quit all social media and live my life to the max. I could reacquaint myself with reality and experience the rush of actual existence on all four of my available cheeks. I could reconnect with my true self, with the real me. And who is the real me, you ask? Well, allow me to introduce myself.

My name is James Acaster but you won't know that because I now have zero social media presence. What do I have instead? A little thing called Life Presence. Want some? Follow me.

The End

First things first, let's get into the science. It's an established fact that every time you open a social media app your phone secretes three things into the air: highly potent sex pheromones, the smell of powdered chocolate and the message, 'This is absolutely fine and you love this' (at a frequency that only owls can hear but the human soul can still absorb). What does this mean? It means you're an addict and a tragic one at that. Now's the time to accept this and start repairing what's left of the human being your friends once knew and, on your good days, loved.

Second things first – this is a book. It's going to take some getting used to because empty-headed Internuts like you won't be familiar. You're gonna want to walk around with it for a while, get used to the weight of it in your stiff little claw hands that have long frozen into the shape of your stupid phones. With any luck, your bony mitts will unthaw over time and you'll regain the dexterity required to turn a physical page. Oh, and when it comes to turning pages you're gonna want to pick up the bottom right corner of the right-hand page between your thumb and forefinger and move it over, in an arcing motion, to your left, until it lies on top of the previous page and becomes the bottom left corner of the left-hand page. If you've done this correctly you should be looking at two new pages by the end. Aggressively swiping left and right will only result in you creasing up the paper (that's what the pages are made of) and you can't zoom in and out of the text with your fingers either. Unless you use your fingers to grip the book and lift the entire thing closer to your actual eyes.

Third things first – congratulations. 99.9 per cent of internet users actually won't have made it this far and those of you who have will know – it's taken you weeks. You had to keep going back to reread sentences because you started thinking about different types of breakfast or David Ginola's hair, maybe you lost concentration and the entire paragraph stopped making comprehensible sense. Getting this far in a book with an easily distracted baby-mind like yours is no small feat and I applaud you for it – you clearly have the determination required to one day give up social media and live a meaningful life worth giving a shit about. But it's gonna take a buttload of work because, right now, you're a stupid idiot who needs to get reacquainted with a little thing called The Real World. But more on that later. For now, I'll just make sure we throw in an attention grabbing word or phrase every now and then in order to help you maintain focus. **PENIS. KARATE.** Welcome back.

There are a few similarities between a book like this and the social media sites you're used to reading, the most obvious being – words. Just like the tweets and statuses you regularly guzzle like a pedal bin full of other people's stale McDonald's, a book is full of written words. This means that you cannot hear the words being uttered out loud so therefore you may misread the tone and the writer's intent may be lost. But, unlike your twitters and your beebos, the text in this book has been written and rewritten over and over again. Countless drafts have been drafted, more than one person has scoured every single word, notes have been given, alterations have occurred, every effort has been made to ensure the writer can most accurately convey exactly what they mean and avoid being misunderstood or misrepresented by rabid junkyard dogs like you. The internet, on the other hand, is a place where everybody, no matter how skilled a writer they are, can have a go at writing and then have their rookie attempts read by literally everybody. So of course it's a disaster. It's like if everybody in the world decided to throw knives at each other regardless of whether they were a professional knife thrower or had ever picked up a knife in their life. Long story short, most of us would end up getting stabbed by our own knives while criticising other people's shitty knife throwing. And if I'm coming across as a judgmental, high and mighty dickhead right now, it's because I intend to and I've made sure of it by redrafting this entire section until it's impossible for the reader to perceive me as anything other than a smug prick. This is how true writing works, bozo, get used to it. **BREASTS. FIRE. ICE CREAM.**

People often ask me, 'James, now that you're off social media, have all of your problems gone away?' and the answer is, always, of course they have. One thing you need to understand is that all of the stress, anxiety, anger, depression, paranoia, sadness, sexual arousal and self-hatred contained within your life come from social media. Some of you will remember what life was like before the internet – carefree, pain-free, serene and euphoric. You never worried about anything and anything never worried about you. Well, I'm here to tell you – those days don't have to be behind you, they're not gone for good. In fact, they never left at all, they're just waiting for you to get back in touch. **SHARKS.**

Before we move on, I'd quickly like to clear something up. I quit social media for the reason we should all quit social media – it's objectively better for our mental health. That's it. I know there are a lot of rumours going around that I quit because that video of me getting my tie caught in a candy floss machine went viral. Or that I quit because that video of me mistakenly biting a small cactus thinking it was a cupcake went viral. Or that I quit because that video of me getting chased by a happy dinosaur football mascot went viral. Or that I quit because that video of me falling asleep on a bucking bronco and not spilling my cheese fries went viral. Or that I quit because that video of me puking out of a hot-air balloon while flying directly over a millionaire's wedding went viral. Or that I quit because that video of me weeping in front of a busker playing an accordion rendition of 'Fix You' went viral. Or that I quit because that video of me being interviewed on the news about the new *DragonBots* movie went viral and I was so excited in the video that everything I said was unintelligible and super high-pitched and to this day I still get people yelling, 'The power of cinema!' at me in falsetto whenever I leave the goddamn house. None of those things have ever bothered me even in the slightest. You don't need to accidentally go viral fifty-seven times in order to leave social media. You just need to aspire to live a better life. And if that better life involves not having embarrassing clips of yourself posted back at you by strangers every waking second of the day then so be it. Just to reiterate – I can totally take a joke and have no problem whatsoever with a single one of those videos. They're good value and if people want to spend the limited time they have on this planet watching videos of someone they don't know messing up in a completely understandable way, then that is up to them. Any laughter at my expense bounces right off me and up into the eternal void of nothingness that is outer space. I quit social media for the exact same reason nicotine addicts quit cigarettes – it's objectively better for your physical health. The fact that, in some people's eyes, I was routinely humiliated online is neither here nor there. **CARS. HURRICANES. PIRATES.** Trust me, I'm fine. **THE MARVEL CINEMATIC UNIVERSE.**

The dangers of the fake profile

Before I tell you how to quit social media, I'm gonna tell you how *not* to quit social media. I know some of you smart-arses think you can find an easy way out, some sort of loophole that means you don't have to 100% quit. Well, I'm here to tell you such a thing only exists in your pitiful little dreams. I bet you think it's a genius idea to delete your online profiles then secretly create a bunch of fake profiles under a pseudonym, enabling you to continue interacting with the world in disguise. Am I right, Einstein? Am I right, Vorderman? You think you're an A+ Oxbridge brainbox, don't you? As far as all your pals are concerned, you've quit social media, you're a real inspiration, a regular Pip the Wonderdog, everyone gives you a huge round of applause and admires the self-control it took to come offline. But the truth is you've only quit by name and that name may as well be Big Old Coward. Behind the scenes, you're still a shivering webhead chasing those dopamine hits under some dumb alias that sounds vaguely like your actual name (e.g. Wig Gold Howard, Pig Mould Mallard or something else that rhymes with Big Old Coward). The fake profile does not work and is way more perilous than you Screenies think it is, and I should know. Or rather, Jaym Baecaster should know.

Twenty-four hours after deleting my MySpace account, I decided to bin the rest of my socials in one fell swoop. I spat on my computer screen after each deletion until I could barely see the 'delete account' icon and it felt incredible. I was convinced that by sheer willpower alone I'd be able to resist ever going back online. But I hadn't counted on my oldest enemy fighting back and trying to keep me trapped in the 'net. No, I'm not talking about Tom – I'm talking about me. My own oldest enemy is myself. Pretty deep, right?

I'd barely been offline a week and already I was Jonesing big time. There are many loopholes the average weakling (like you) will try to utilise during the first few weeks of kicking the cyber habit. Even without a profile, searching your name on Twitter is extremely common, especially if you're a celebrity – as I am and will be until the day I die. I shamefully admit that after quitting Twitter I used to search 'James Acaster' numerous times throughout the day. Don't get me wrong, the very act of searching 'James Acaster' online isn't anything to be ashamed of. Most people search those very words during their lifetime, in fact it's one of the most popular web searches out there. It only adopts a tinge of sadness when the person searching 'James Acaster' is James Acaster himself and, as James Acaster, that's the position I found myself in. The reason I searched my own name was because I wanted to see what people were saying about me, and I was surprised/gutted to discover that nobody tweeted about me whatsoever. Nobody, that is, except for @tangerinejill – an older woman who would regularly tweet about wanting to taste my 'golden syrup locks'. You didn't misread that and I didn't mistype it. I tried not to judge Tangerine Jill but it was hard not to when she routinely tweeted, 'Wondering what my baby James Acaster's golden syrup locks taste like today', usually accompanied by close-up images of my hair on various UK panel shows. But who was I to judge Tangerine Jill when I, the very man whose hair she wanted to taste, was searching my own name every day and reading all of her tweets, including the ones that didn't even mention me because I wanted to get a feel for the woman outside of her desire to taste my golden syrup locks. I wasn't enjoying this ghostly existence: being able to see Tangerine Jill's tweets about me, experiencing a visceral reaction to them but having nowhere to direct my energy because I was profile-less and therefore incapable of responding to the Tangerine Jills of the world. Some of you are probably thinking, *What you should do is rejoin Twitter so you can engage with this Tangerine Jill character and settle this hair consumption business once and for all.* Hahaha. Wrong as always, doofuses (doofi?). Watch and learn. Or rather, read and learn. Or listen and learn if you've bought the audiobook. Either way – get ready to learn.

If I rejoined Twitter as James Acaster, then I was letting the internet, and all of its dumbass users (including you), win. Let's say this book inspires you and you finally do the sensible thing and leave Twitter. The entire world has seen you delete your profile, so if you come back to Twitter after an all-too-brief hiatus, you'll look pathetic. Like you thought you were too good for the site and now you're admitting you're just as feeble as everyone else on there. It's not a good look. So I decided to show everyone how not-pathetic I was by doing the least pathetic thing ever – creating a fake profile and calling myself Jaym.

Jaym Baecaster

Jaym Baecaster was a no-nonsense, fun-loving scientist who loved Crowded House, pasta and scaling a climbing wall on his days off. How did I land on this specific set of characteristics? I borrowed them from a little person known as Tangerine Jill. The whole point of creeping back onto Twitter was to get to the bottom of who this Tangerine Jill character was, so I copied and pasted all of her interests, immediately giving myself an in when it came to striking up a conversation with this hair-obsessed lunatic. The plan was simple: head over to Tangerine Jill's profile, bond over our shared interests (wink), then ask her why exactly she wanted to taste this James Acaster guy's hair. I have never in my entire life experienced anything as straightforward as getting Tangerine Jill to respond to me. I think it's safe to say, Tangerine Jill wasn't getting @ed in many strangers' tweets. So when @JaymBaecaster5 hollered at her out of nowhere, asking if she preferred penne or fusilli, old Tangerine Jill responded within seconds: 'I'm Team Fusilli but omg have you tried strozzapreti?!'

It was so tempting to ask if she liked angel hair pasta but I resisted as I didn't want to reveal my intentions straight out the gate. I replied saying I loved strozzapreti (never even tried it, don't know what it is) before adding that strozzapreti was also the go-to pasta of Crowded House alumnus Nick Seymour (no idea if that's even true, made it up). Naturally, Tangerine Jill went ga-ga for this little tidbit and our 'friendship' was well and truly cemented (obviously, after my MySpace ordeal, the word friendship meant jack shit to me so I didn't care about misleading Tangerine Jill when it came to such meaningless endeavours). For the next few days, I spent every waking hour on Twitter chatting to Tangerine Jill about anything and everything. It wasn't long before I got bombarded with messages and friend requests from Tangerine Jill's online peers. The T-JOPs (Tangerine Jill's Online Peers) also loved science, climbing, pasta and Crowded House but, most of all, they loved Jaym Baecaster. In a single thread, I got to discuss Italian cuisine, particle physics and middle-of-the-road nineties soft rock – three subjects I knew nothing about but managed to blag my way through by copying and pasting passages from Wikipedia and adding the phrase 'in my humble opinion' at the end.

It was unexpected but Jaym was giving me the opportunity to learn more about the world whilst engaging with some genuinely fascinating people, all of whom I'd tricked into liking me. But my blissful patch lasted all of two days before I started to attract people who disagreed with Jaym; people who hated pasta so much it made them hurl and dreamt of 'Don't Dream It's Over' finally being over. And so it was that most of my time as Jaym Baecaster was spent defending subjects I knew nothing about against people I knew less than nothing about. With every slagging match, I felt the line between my online life and my real life begin to blur. I started up Jaym Baecaster accounts on Facebook, Instagram, Snapchat and LinkedIn. I even started a Baecaster MySpace account, becoming the first new MySpace user in over a decade. The five existing MySpace users quickly grew to dislike Baecaster as he kept requesting that Arctic Monkeys cover Crowded House songs and would troll one user in particular within an inch of his sad, steak-munching, travelling-salesjerk life. Tom let Baecaster know that he was an unwelcome presence on MySpace but was unable to ban him from the site as they badly needed the numbers. I wish I could give you more detail here but memories of that time are hazy because they aren't mine – they're Baecaster's. Whenever I wasn't online, I still found myself thinking like him. One afternoon I was doing some crate digging at my local record store (no, crate digging isn't what I needed to buy a spade for, lol) when I overheard someone slagging off the album *Together Alone*. I flipped my lid, called them a brainless poser, bit my thumb at them and am no longer welcome at Big Jack's Track Shack. One evening, I straight-up yelled at a stranger for choosing Mexican over Italian food at a world cuisine buffet. My behaviour was disproportionate at best and I am no longer welcome at Gluttonous Gladys's Global Gobblers. I once found myself sitting in a lecture about string theory (my feet just kind of walked me there) and challenged the tutor on quantum chromodynamics, confidently writing an equation on the chalkboard, Will Hunting style. Obviously, I'd written a load of gobbledegook nonsense up there but no one questioned any of it because I carried myself in a way that let people know it wasn't worth it.

As if all this concerning behaviour wasn't bad enough, I was also beginning to forget details of my own life. The likes and dislikes I'd committed to my social media profiles all those years ago gradually flickered into nothingness, getting replaced by the details of my new *fake* profiles, until one day I woke up and James Acaster was nowhere to be seen. That's right, I'd stopped dreaming and it was indeed over. I know I've referenced that song twice now but it's the only Crowded House track any of you philistines will have heard of. Case in point, I referenced *Together Alone* earlier and you didn't know what the fuck I was on about so get off my back. What I'm trying to say is, I woke up one morning, I didn't dream and, for James Acaster at least, it was over. I'd gone full Baecaster.

Full Baecaster

My wardrobe, inspired by the selfies posted by Tangerine Jill, became strictly black and cream and consisted of skinny jeans, baggy woollen jumpers, humongous boots and that hat that Pharrell wore once. I was eating spaghetti and meatballs three times a day, listening to Neil Finn's back catalogue on shuffle, and picking fights with Christians more or less round the clock. I flooded my flat with science equipment: bunsen burners, stethoscopes, a big metal ball where if you touch it your hair stands on end and a second big metal ball in case more than one person wanted to do the hair thing at the same time. As Baecaster, I became the first person to receive a loyalty card for Frankie & Benny's and, for your information, I made bloody good use of it. Put it this way, I was as loyal to Frankie & Benny's as Frankie was to Benny. The less said about Benny's loyalty to Frankie the better. The guy's a scumbag. During my time as Jaym, I went to see Crowded House tribute act Cramped Bungalow a total of thirty-two times and if it was sold out I'd always make the same joke to the person squashed in next to me and they never once laughed. As much as I loved the band, Crowded House fans were hardly a barrel of giggles and, in the end, this proved to be my undoing.

My most memorable day as Jaym Baecaster was the time I got into an argument with a fellow Crowded House fan online who insisted that Liam Finn was a better musician than Neil Finn. I had long forgotten about Tangerine Jill and now lived to argue, even if it was with people from my own tribe. This particular Crowded House fan had found me after I'd tweeted about wanting to taste Neil Finn's golden syrup locks, replying with, 'I'd much rather slurp down Liam Finn's honeysuckle barnet.' Which enraged me. I challenged this so-called fan and our tweets got so heated that Liam himself intervened and told us to 'just enjoy the music'. The argument got so out of hand that Chunky Duncan (the user's username) demanded we meet in person and settle this once and for all. Now, normally I would never agree to something like this – I'm James Acaster, a meek, retiring fellow who fears confrontation – but Jaym Baecaster loves a good scrap. I accepted immediately and told Chunky Duncan to be in the car park of Frankie & Benny's in twenty-five minutes (I was already in Frankie & Benny's itself, waiting on some microwaved penne). Twenty-five minutes later, I dabbed the corners of my mouth with a napkin, got my loyalty card stamped and strode outside, ready to rumble. But when my feet touched the tarmac, I looked around and couldn't see Chunky Duncan anywhere. Instead I was met with the sight of a much more familiar face – the face of my father. The old grey bear. My eyes drifted past my dad's bald head to see my mother, my siblings and my entire extended family huddled next to a speed bump – this wasn't a car park scrap, this was an intervention. I'd been tricked in the most thoughtful way imaginable! My loved ones sat me down in a mother and child parking bay and took it in turns to explain to me how Jaym Baecaster was affecting their wellbeing. His heckles had ruined my cousin's baptism, the climbing wall he'd built in my parent's garden was a health and safety nightmare, and playing the same song at every single funeral was beginning to wear thin (plus the lyrics were 'too on the nose'). My family showed me Baecaster's online activity and it was like reading the diary of a psychopath. I didn't recognise the person who said those things. Sure, I thought it was pretty great he bullied Ernie Freedman but outside of that, the guy was out of line. I had to face facts – Jaym had to go. I handed over my login details to my bald father, my mother tore up my loyalty card (I was two stamps away from a free garlic bread, thanks Mum) and I've been James Acaster ever since (with the exception of my music taste, I still listen exclusively to the rockingest band in the Southern Hemisphere and make no apologies).

So there you have it! That's the story of how I totally quit social media and turned my life around. It honestly couldn't have been more straightforward! I hope you found my story helpful and that one day you too can come offline for good. You can do it! Just believe in yourself and anything is possible!

Take care of yourselves and remember – you're awesome.

Peace, love and understanding.

Sincerely,

James x

Fin.

PSYCH! Did you really think it'd be that easy, you chumps?! This is the real world and in the real world there are ups and downs, you chumps. The end of that Jaym Baecaster story may have sounded like a happy ending but in reality it resulted in me falling head first off the wagon and into a big old puddle of cloudy horse excreta. Pay close attention to what happened next and take heed. Heed my words. In fact, heed this entire book. Everything I say here should be heeded and heed should be taken from it. If this is the first portion of heed you've taken from this book then I recommend starting again. You left some heed back in the earlier pages and you gotta take it with you. OK – heed this next bit.

The Relapse

After my family revealed how much they'd missed me during my Baecaster phase, I decided to rejoin all social media under my own name, reconnect with the Acasters and show them how much they meant to me.

I KNOW, I KNOW. It seems like an obvious mistake in hindsight, sure. But in regular sight, I just wanted to do something nice for my mum.

The only website I didn't rejoin was MySpace. My family weren't on there and I didn't fancy returning in the wake of Baecaster. Baecaster had essentially gone on MySpace, got everyone's hopes up that the site was popular again, reigned carnage and then quit. The vibe was sure to be even bleaker than usual and I did not fancy a slice of that bleak pie. Also, they had no idea I'd been Baecaster so showing up shortly after he'd left, as myself, might be a tad suspicious. I doubt I could pull off a convincing, 'Hey guys! Did I miss anything?' without immediately getting busted.

Yep, I had to swerve MySpace but my interactions with family and friends on all other social media platforms went wonderfully. I liked all their photos, left nice comments on their walls and all was well in Internet Land once more.

BUT THAT'S HOW THEY GET YA.

Thanks to my nearest and bloody dearest, I became a full-on Screeny again, my thumbs growing more hench than the rest of me combined. I'm talking a stark difference, thumb to body wise. The rest of me had all but wasted away while my thumbs could comfortably flip over a parked truck. I knew I had a problem when I found myself saying, to my reflection in my laptop screen, 'What has two gigantic thumbs and needs to quit social media? This guy!' before bursting into laughter, then tears, then song – the main three things a human being can burst into, the fourth being flames. Also the song was the British national anthem and I don't know why.

These were confusing times but I knew this much: I needed to figure out some sort of exit strategy and it *had to be* more robust than last time. Losing myself during the Jaym Baecaster episode had really shaken me and I knew I couldn't just delete my profiles and expect to be cured overnight. Systems needed to be put in place and things had to be done the <u>right</u> way. I reflected on my initial attempt to leave, trying to see where I'd gone wrong, and one cock up was immediately apparent. It wasn't something I'd done but, rather, something I'd neglected to do. Something embarrassingly obvious, in fact. The more I thought about it, the more I laughed at my own oversight. I'm laughing right now just remembering it. None of you will have spotted it but luckily I'm here to guide you through the murky corridors of the 'net and up towards the light. It's blatant as hell and if you still haven't figured it out yet, all you have to do is ask yourself one simple question:

How can you leave if you don't say goodbye?

Saying Goodbye

Newsflash, chumps! Before you officially delete any social media accounts you must issue an official statement on said accounts saying you officially won't be there any more. I know that years of wasting each other online has turned you into the rudest trashbags who ever walked this dump of a planet but it doesn't hurt to employ a little courtesy before saying sayonara. You have to bid the internet a proper and meaningful farewell. The best place to do this is Facebook.

There's something about Facebook that feels more personal than Twitter or Instagram. Twitter is where you post all your shitty opinions and Instagram is where you make out your life is perfect. But Facebook enables you to combine your shitty opinions and the misleading photos – giving everyone a fuller picture of your truest self. Now, before you begin mindlessly tapping away at your keyboard, farting out an amatuer toodle-oo to all of humanity – there's a right way and there's a wrong way to write a final status. You can't just go full pedal to the metal and type out a stream of consciousness full of whatever goop is drifting around your lava lamp of a noggin. That approach always leads to self-glorification and, believe it or not, this isn't just about you. Funerals aren't for the deceased – they're for those left behind. So stop behaving like a selfish wanker and take a moment to consider the community you're about to plunge into a state of mourning.

I myself went through many drafts before I settled on my final words, experimenting with various tones and even adopting different personas. There was a draft where I tried to guilt everyone into feeling like me leaving was their fault. There was a draft where I called social media a cesspool and tried shaming everybody for contributing to it. There was a draft where I told everyone to go fuck themselves. But none of these iterations quite struck the appropriate chord. In the end I settled on the following *very carefully* chosen set of words. What I present to you now is from my now-deceased Facebook account. May it rot forever in Hell:

Hello 'Friends',

Just jumping on here to let you know that this'll be my final status on this 'site'. As of midnight tonight I will be deleting all of my social media accounts across all platforms.

I will be back on Facebook several times between now and the termination of my account to check up on how this status is doing and liking any positive comments from people supporting my decision to leave. Comments aren't the be all and end all, of course, just fifty or so 'likes' would do me fine. This whole 'leaving social media' thing is only a positive decision if I'm going to be missed so please, let me know I'm not making a massive mistake. You have between now and midnight.

Anyway, I don't want to end my final status grovelling for 'likes' from a bunch of arseholes. I want to end on an emotional note. OK, here it comes.

The world is a big and beautiful place and it's waiting for each and every one of you, somewhere beyond your screens. We've only got one life – do you really want to spend it staring at your phone? I know some of you believe we have more than one life but I think my point stands regardless. Like, if there is an afterlife, won't you feel pretty stupid when you get there and you have to admit to your god that you spent your Earth life just looking at your phone all the time? What if there are phones in the afterlife and you end up spending eternity staring at your afterlife phone? Does *that* sound nice to you? Maybe you'll be reincarnated as a different animal and will be unable to stare at a phone because you're a goat now. That one sounds nice actually. I guess if reincarnation is real then it's OK to spend this life staring at your phone because you get a whole second life as a goat not even knowing what a phone is so it balances out.

Ignoring the goat thing, whatever way you slice it, social media is robbing us of our lives, it's robbing us of feeling alive and it's robbing us of our *afterlives* (maybe). If you don't quit today, then when? If not you, then who? If not how, then why? If not no, then yes.

It's been a crazy ride, guys, thanks for all the memories and thanks for all the love. Life is for living and love is for loving xx

You're all idiots,

James

No one sent any likes.

. . .

From that day forth, I can honestly say, I have never so much as glanced at a single social media site ever again. I made a plan and I stuck to it. I posted my final status and followed every step I'd carefully laid out all the way to freedom.

But what were those steps, you ask? How did I do it? How did I go from being Jaym Baecaster to quitting multiple social media sites and living to tell the tale? Well, let me ask you this:

you're in a polyamorous relationship with multiple partners but they're all doing your head in – how do you break up with them all at the same time? Do you tell them all at once? Do you tell them individually? Do you repeat the same break-up technique with each person? Or do you break up with each individual using an efficient break-up method specifically catered for their personality type? The answer is yes.

The initial cull

It's all well and good posting an official goodbye but you need to follow it up with a little thing called 'action'.

I'd tried everything over the years: limiting my screen time on my phone, deleting my social media apps . . . Those were the two things I tried. But in both cases I got around the issue by accessing the sites via my web browser. It became clear to me that if I was going to kick this vile habit once and for all I'd have to go cold turkey. So far, I'd gone warm turkey and occasionally drifted back into hot turkey but now I needed to stick a turkey in the deep freeze and remove the word 'defrost' from my, and the turkey's, vocabulary. Here's how I did it and also how you should do it too.

FACEBOOK
It didn't feel great but I knew the only way to remove the temptation of returning to Facebook was to burn all my bridges with my Facebook friends, not just online but in real life (my real-life friends, not my real-life bridges. That drawbridge cost a pretty penny, I wasn't about to set fire to it just so my aunt can't talk to me). What followed were some extremely dark days.

I did and said a lot of messed-up shit to a lot of good-hearted people, all of whom I care deeply about, and I don't think I can ever take any of it back. I locked my bald dad in an aviary, I recited a close friend's entire gruesome search history during a best man speech, I egged my cousin's private gondola on his birthday, I deliberately put my niece in a *Home Alone* situation, I sold my mum's microscooter to a thrill seeker without her knowledge and I framed my sister for egging my cousin's private gondola on his birthday. I spent an entire morning throwing water balloons at kids on their way to school, all of whom were children of my Facebook friends. It was the first day of school too, so their uniforms were brand new, and I'd filled the water balloons with honey. Anyway, thanks to those malicious and unforgivable acts, I can never show my mug on Facebook ever again. If I had the gall to create a new profile, I'd be universally blocked within seconds, no one would accept my friend requests (apparently, my old Facebook friends have gone out of their way to warn other users about me) and my timeline would be a barren wasteland, full of targeted ads for honey and little else. My Facebook days are officially over. Also, I pushed my uncle in a river.

TWITTER

When it came to Twitter, there was only one thing for it – I had to get myself banned. Nothing else was going to keep me off that site because I was hopelessly hooked on reading short things. I knew I had to say something so offensive, so irredeemable, so effed up, that the Twitter gods would be forced to ban me for life. This took longer than I expected. Much longer. I'll say it, it was actually amazing how long I was able to get away with saying abhorrent stuff on Twitter for. Irresponsible tweet after irresponsible tweet, 148 characters of pure hatred and poisonous bile posted again and again, but nothing – no repercussions, no consequences, just crazy uncut freedom (for me and my frankly dangerous ideas). Sure, I got cancelled a bunch of times but I found a way around that – I simply ignored the cancelling, logged on to the site the following day and said whatever I wanted like the cancelling never happened. Turns out cancelling only counts if the person accepts the cancelling. If they choose to ignore it and carry on as normal, there is absolutely nothing the people who tried to cancel them can do about it. Still, I needed to be stopped – badly – even I was offended by my tweets at this point, for God's sake, they were making me sick and I'd had enough of them.

Eventually the people in charge of Twitter started putting exclamation marks on my tweets to warn people I was full of shit. A good start but still not what I was going for. I had to keep upping the ante. After the exclamation marks, they started adding question marks, so I upped the ante again and Twitter had to get creative. After the question mark, they started using a frowny face emoji to show their displeasure. After the frowny face came a GIF of Dwayne 'The Rock' Johnson aggressively wagging his finger and saying 'uh uh'. Finally, after what felt like a lifetime, Twitter sent a letter home to my parents and banned me from the site. I have no idea what the letter said because, thanks to my antics when leaving Facebook, the olds and I are hardly on speaking terms, but I imagine it doesn't paint me in the best light considering what I did. I'm not even sure I care to admit the thing that got me banned as I don't think I've ever been less proud of anything in my entire life. Let's just say, sometimes it's easier to get a light bulb *into* your mouth than it is to get it out.

Right? No?

Well, let's just say, I spent a long time in hospital having a light bulb removed from my mouth by a team of doctors.

Too specific?

OK, let's just say, I encouraged people to copy the lightbulb thing and a lot of people got hurt thanks to me and if you're one of those people who took part in the hashtag lightbulb challenge and you're reading this book because you're looking for answers, something that explains why you went through what you went through that day, then I hope this explanation helps you put the past behind you where it belongs and push forward with your life. I also hope you have regained use of your jaw. I got lucky and made a full recovery within twenty-four hours but according to my surgeon, this is virtually unheard of. Extra apologies to those of you who opted for the hashtag lightbulbasschallenge as, from what I understand, you got it a lot worse.

God bless you all.

SNAPCHAT

How do you rid yourself of an addiction to looking at random photos very briefly? It was a tough riddle to crack but I managed to come up with a failsafe solution known as Reverse Clockwork Orange Torture.

The subject (in this case, me) is straitjacketed and made to stare at a series of images on a screen. At this point, the subject's eyelids are pinned open by a pair of tiny metal arms. Sound familiar? Well, there's a twist! Every ten seconds the tiny metal arms forcibly close the subject's eyelids before swiftly pinning them open again, presenting the subject with an entirely new image each time. This repeats for hours until the idea of being shown random photos very briefly doesn't seem like awesome fun any more.

I know this sounds unpleasant and you're probably thinking you'll skip this one but that is not an option. You need to ditch every form of social media if you're ever going to get clean and if this particular step sounds unpleasant then guess what – it's torture, it ain't meant to be nice. The clue is in the name, folks.

Bit of advice for anyone considering Reverse Clockwork Orange Torture – get someone else to assist you. I did the whole thing solo and didn't foresee how difficult putting on my own straightjacket would be, let alone positioning metal arms under my eyelids while straitjacketed, handlessly switching on a projector, switching on a second device that moves said metal arms, then somehow switching everything off and freeing myself at the end.

In retrospect, I should've quit Snapchat *before* burning all my bridges with my Facebook friends. Any one of those guys would've gladly helped me out with a little Reverse Clockwork Orange Torture. But at the end of the day, I survived the procedure with only minimal scratches to my cornea and a new weird thing that my arm does sometimes. So, just like the guy in *Clockwork Orange*, I ain't complaining.

TIKTOK

The only advice I can give when it comes to quitting TikTok is to never join it in the first place. Those of you who have already joined – bad luck. I don't know what to tell you. I guess you just shouldn't have joined TikTok and that's on you.

I got off social media just before TikTok blew up and never sampled its sweet, moreish nectar. If you are on TikTok and want to quit, I guess my best advice would be to seek out a hypnotist who can put you in a trance and erase all memory of TikTok from your addled mind. From what I can tell, this is your only hope of not being gakked on tok for the rest of your days. I, personally, still don't have the faintest idea what a TikTok is. I've not even researched it for this book in case I get hooked from the description alone. Also, research is for people who aren't clever enough to figure stuff out by themselves. I'm proud to announce I've done zero research whatsoever for this entire book and all the wisdom contained herein comes from my own once-in-a-generation brain – an Acaster Original.

When it comes to 'what TikTok is', my best guess would be that the site is either clock- or bomb-related since all I've got to go on is its embarrassing, baby-sounding name. I would wager that TikTok users have a limited amount of time to complete statuses or else their account promptly detonates. A countdown accompanies every action, meaning users often rush things, thus increasing the potential for accidental scandals due to ill-thought-out statements being made against the clock. If that's not what it is, and I'm pretty sure it isn't, then someone should create that site. I may be social media free these days but I know a cash cow when I see one. I suppose some might view numerous users getting constantly suspended every day as a negative but, by the end, the website would be solely populated by the cream of the crop. And when I say cream of the crop, I'm talking fast thinkers and even faster typers. Essentially, you'd be left with a large volume of politically sound touch typists. Yes. Please. The coolest of the cool.

Full disclosure, I might invent this site. Obviously, I'll call it something besides TikTok. ClockWork? Yes. No. No, no, no. This is the kind of thinking that gets me in trouble.

Self-Imposed Rule 204: no creating my own social media sites as a way of re-entering social media.

If it wasn't for Self-Imposed Rule 204, I'd be back on social media 24/7 (literally), making friends on *CrashMat* or *Slinky* or *ToastFlip* or *Satchel* or *PopRock* or *Turtle* or *TopDrawer* or *Libra* or *SuperOnlineFriendshipCity* or *PinDrop* or *Nub* or *UpDown* or *Barber* or *WingSpan* or *Trudger* or *HopHop* or *Quilt* or *ClingFilm* or *Gibraltar* or *PaddlingPool* or *Denzel* or any number of sites that I've already invented, patented and then thought better of. Any one of those could have made me a trillionaire but my sanity comes first so in the trash they go or, more accurately, into a folder labelled 'Last Resort' they go and hopefully I'll never need to open it. Oh, and when I say 'trash' and 'folder', I'm not talking about my computer, I'm talking about a real-life bin and a real-life cardboard folder I bought from Ryman's. Not only have I gone social media free, I've gone 100% computer free also . . . but more on that later. Anyway, referring to my wastepaper basket as the 'trash' is the only ugly hangover from my 'desktop days' and I'd thank you not to mock me for it.

INSTAGRAM

This was tough. All in all, Instagram was a pleasant affair and my only gripe was that I spent too much time on there looking at awesome photos of ice cream (just typing that made me salivate). Did I compare my life to the lives of my fellow Instagrammers? Yes. But that's why I only followed people who lived exactly the same life as me. That way, every time they posted something, I'd just comment 'same' and continue with my day feeling seen (as well as heard, felt, smelt and tasted). Under normal circumstances, I would never quit something that boosted my self-esteem and showed me images of mind-blowing ice cream from around the world, but I had made a deal with myself – I had to quit ALL social media – which meant Insta had to go in the Binsta (not much better than saying 'trash' but at least it rhymes).

I feel I should be honest here. More than any other social media platform, quitting this one felt impossible. No matter how hard I tried, I kept finding new loopholes, new excuses, anything to keep looking at photos of delicious Neapolitan ice cream, wafers and all. I was running out of ideas and so, after many failed attempts to quit Instagram, I finally did something I should've done a long time ago. I painted over my phone screen with tar.

Problem solved.

Don't worry, I also pierced the camera lens with a tin opener in case I attempted to take photos blind.

Problem solved.

OK, maybe not problem 100% solved, actually

Despite painting over the screen of my phone with tar, I had hoped my touch screen would function through said tar and I'd still be able to accept phone calls, albeit from a slew of mystery callers – but I was wrong. It turns out tar is thick as fat treacle and twice as sticky. In short, my phone was now useless and may as well have been a shit drinks coaster. I thought about replacing it with a new phone but knew that such a thing would only lure me back over to the dark side. If you were trying to give up caffeine and (inexplicably) made the decision to buy an espresso machine, then proceeded to carry that espresso machine around with you all day long, taking it with you as you walked around your home from room to room, maybe even taking the espresso machine into the toilet with you and never leaving the house without said espresso machine in your bag – what do you think is maybe going to happen? You are correct. Sooner or later, you're going to drink an espresso. And guess what? Not a living soul on this planet will be surprised when you do. So that's why I refused to buy a new phone.

I bid farewell to any future calls or text messages and I redirected my faith towards the trusty Royal Mail, despite the fact that my postman hated delivering letters to me. Which I totally empathised with, by the way. My house had a god-damn drawbridge instead of a door, for crying out loud, and drawbridges don't come fitted with letterboxes. Oh, and in case you're wondering – no, I still hadn't got a moat dug. The drawbridge had been standing firm since '03, we've established that. But I never got round to digging the moat thanks to my seventeen-year-long social media addiction. It wasn't until coming off social media that I even remembered I'd needed to dig a moat in the first place. I made a note to resume Project Moat ASAP even though I was fairly certain that the sudden arrival of a moat around my house would make my postman despise me even more.

Some of you may now be thinking, *Hold on, James, you're telling me you were buying a drawbridge for your own house before MySpace even existed? Surely, you weren't old enough to be doing such a thing back in those days.* Well, I'll have you know I was eighteen years old at the time in question and there's a little tradition in the Acaster family whereby on your eighteenth birthday you build and move into your own castle.

The surname 'Acaster' is Olden Speak for 'Castle Master', meaning my ancestors built all the castles back in olden times and, fun fact, are the only people still legally allowed to build castles wherever we like today – as long as we're of age. Long before I cut all ties with my family in order to quit Facebook, I had already let them all down by becoming the first Acaster not to complete their debut castle. All I had done was buy a detached house, swap the front door for a drawbridge and acquire a social media addiction, halting Project Castle in its tracks. No moat, no turrets, no towers, no weird narrow slits in the walls that people can fire arrows through. I had officially brought shame on the Acaster name by being 'a lazy sod' (in the words of my very bald father).

Project Moat was the first step to repairing the damage social media had done to my life over the years. If I could complete my castle, I could prove to the world that the old ways are still the best ways.

Even more of you may now be thinking, *We want to copy your methods when it comes to quitting Instagram but where do we get tar from?*

Excellent question. I suggest you do what I did and make friends with a local road worker. They're easily found due to the amount of hi-vis they wear, but getting close enough to them to form a friendship can be tricky. Their place of work is usually out of bounds on account of all the health and safety hazards, i.e. potholes, boiling tar and wolves, so if you want to befriend a road worker you're going to need to become a cement mixer salesman. There's literally no other way to start a conversation with these guys – you need to have something they want and then they'll come to you. I invested in ten high quality cement mixers and travelled the United Kingdom selling them to the highest bidder. Strictly speaking, you should have a set price, but I found it more fun to have the road workers barter with me. Plus it's not like I knew how much they were meant to cost anyway. Over the course of selling cement mixers, you should expect to make friends with at least one road worker. For me it was Demetri, an unusual (creepy) fella who kept saying the cement mixer I'd sold him reminded him of an affable banshee he conversed with as a child. Once you've made friends with a road worker, you need to gradually build up to asking them for some tar. I put hours of work into this, going to the cinema with Demetri, out to restaurants, football matches, his sister's wedding, then asked if he could hook me up with a jar of tar on the one-month anniversary of our friendship (which we celebrated by attending an illegal sumo fight). This might sound like a lot of work but once you've burned all your bridges with everyone you know, it's nice to find a new friend and scratch each other's backs every once in a while. You'll also need a paintbrush to paint over your phone with but you can buy those from any arts and crafts shop – there's no need to befriend a portrait artist or decorator, you'll be half-pleased to hear (which half is up to you).

It did later occur to me that painting over my phone screen with tar would've solved *all* my social media problems, not just my Instagram problem, and I should've just painted over my phone with tar in the first place. If I'd thought of painting over my phone with tar sooner I'd still have functioning eyelids and an existing relationship with my parents. But we live and learn. Once I had painted over my phone with tar, I decided to go all in and paint over my laptop screen with tar also. I had to put in a few more hours with Demetri but once we'd attended a murder mystery night together, he was more than happy to part with another warm jar of thick, buttery road tar.

Two reasons for extending the tar-painting to my laptop:

1) I could access social media on my laptop and knew that if I didn't paint over my laptop screen with tar then it was only a matter of time before I was carrying my laptop around with me, hooked up to a portable battery, permanently open, permanently being held in both my hands, no matter how much of an inconvenience that would inevitably become.

2) I realised I didn't just hate social media, I hated the entire internet. The more I thought about it, the more it made sense. I was spending every waking hour online. If I wasn't on social media, I was on my emails or watching funny cow videos on YouTube or reading Pete Sampras's regular fashion blogs, and it was this constant need to be staring at a screen, flooding every nook and cranny of my brain with endorphins, that made me want to quit social media in the first place. It wasn't that I didn't like all the things that social media gave me because I bloody LOVED them. Don't have a bad word to say about them, actually. I just hated the fact I didn't have an actual three-dimensional life any more. Plus all that screen staring was making my brain feel glum. I would be kidding myself if I believed that getting rid of social media would stop me being online non-stop. So I painted over my phone *and* my laptop with a generous helping of tar (thank you, Demetri, much obliged) and put them both in a storage container in North Wales.

Rhyll

I needed to put my devices far enough away that the trip alone would put me off retrieving them in the future. Don't get me wrong, I did have a lovely time in Rhyll, the staff at the Fill 'Em Up, Rhyll 'Em Up self-storage centre were very nice, but I knew I'd never go back because a) it was a massive trek and b) in 2011 I supported Milton Jones on tour in Rhyll and got brutally heckled for the duration of my set. 2011 might sound like a long time ago but almost a decade later, when I put my devices in storage, every local not only remembered the gig but wasn't shy about bringing it up to my face. On my way into Rhyll 'Em Up, a young chap on a bicycle yelled, 'What you collecting, Acaster? Your dignity?' I wanted to inform him that I wasn't 'collecting' anything, I was depositing something, but I doubt that would've done me any favours. Also, the chap in question was about thirteen which meant he hadn't even started primary school when I did the original nightmare Rhyll gig – he clearly only knew about it because it'd become local legend. There was absolutely no way I would ever be returning to Rhyll.

If you're wondering – yes, *you* also have to put your phone and laptop in a storage container in Rhyll. Unless you live in Rhyll or the surrounding area, then it's not far enough away. My advice would be, choose somewhere you can't be bothered to travel to, check they've got a storage centre and book your-self a container. Always check they've got a storage centre in advance otherwise you are going to be livid when you arrive and there's fuck all there. No trying to wriggle out of painting over your laptop screen with tar either. Just accept it's for the best, slap on a smile and lather on the tar.

Usually, getting taunted by a child on a bicycle would ruin my day but, thanks to severing the connection between myself and the World Wide Wasteland, I was in a sparkling mood on the train to London from horrible Rhyll. Had I still been online, I'm sure I would have tweeted about my ordeal, recounting the verbal abuse I'd just received on a Welsh street, in the hopes of being comforted by strangers. As it was, I just sat there as the train trundled on and felt free, like I was gazing into a glittering new dawn, knowing it didn't matter that I couldn't tweet about my ordeal because I would one day be able to vent about that little shit in my very own book. I alighted the train at Euston with a spring in my step, bought myself a spade on the way home (without the help of MySpade.com, thank you very much) and began the first chapter in my new life – a life full of draw*bridges* but not draw*backs*.

Sidenote: MySpade.com wouldn't have been of any use anyway. I'm told it's been bought out by, drum roll please, Tom Space of MySpace. MySpade.com now purely consists of a single page redirecting people to MySpace.com and that's it. If you want to buy a spade online you'll have to visit TrowelsNotTrolls.org and hope for the best.

Drawback number one

There was one small drawback when it came to painting over the screen of my phone with tar, piercing the camera lens with a tin opener and putting it in a storage container in Rhyll and I feel I should reveal it to you in the interest of full disclosure. I did start to miss taking photographs. This will happen to you too so best prepare for it now. The ability to document my life photographically was something I'd taken full advantage of over the years. I would photograph every meal, every band I saw live, every weird-looking stranger on public transport (secretly), but most of all, I would photograph myself, AKA I would take a James.

Those who can't think for themselves call them selfies (as in 'I can't think for my-selfie') but I'm a firm believer in identity and believe we should all refer to selfies as our own names; it means more. I would take a James wherever I went so that I could look back and remember the time I visited a new place and took loads of Jameses there. People would say I was spoiling the experience for myself, that I'd end up with no memories to look back on because all I did was take Jameses all day. Wrong. I have *loads* of memories to look back on precisely *because* I took Jameses all day. All those snobs who walked round the Sistine Chapel taking in everything and not snapping a single Them only have their unreliable snob-brains for memories. I have 100% accurate Jameses. I can look at a James and see myself standing in the Sistine Chapel in a photo also taken by myself. If anything, as both photographer and subject, I couldn't be *more* involved in the moment. Plus I can now experience the photograph of the moment for the rest of my life – the moment never ends and I win forever.

Photographs became the first thing I missed when quitting social media. Without the ability to document everything constantly, I started forgetting things: meals I'd eaten, entire holidays, air hockey matches with Demetri. I had no way of knowing what I'd done without the evidence to prove it. I can't even tell you whether or not I visited the Sistine Chapel during that time because I didn't have a James to confirm it for me. Unphotographed food tasted disgusting, unphotographed bands sounded like garbage, unphotographed weirdos on public transport made me feel threatened or sad. I needed to start capturing things again or there was a strong chance my entire life would escape me.

For this reason, my next step for surviving life outside of social media is simple and plain – buy a camera.

Photography

All you World Wide Wankers probably don't know this, but cameras do exist outside of camera phones. Although, against all logic, they're actually *bigger* when bought on their own. I can't quite wrap my head around this and strongly suggest you don't even try – I'm not a scientist and you're barely a lab assistant. I didn't want a massive camera. I searched forever, but the only camera-phone-sized-cameras I could find turned out to be actual camera phones. Surely, once you've taken a camera phone and got rid of all the social media, texts, phone calls, games, calculators, notes, weather apps, music, voice memos and food delivery services, the remaining bit that's a camera must be the size of a baby's fingernail. But no. I bought a camera, on its own, and it was the size of at least thirty iPhones (stacked fifteen high and two wide). The first thing I took a photograph of was the final cement mixer I'd failed to sell when befriending road workers. It'd become quite the centrepiece in my bedroom, positioned at the foot of my bed, the open drum facing me as I tried to sleep. I would often turn the mixer on and it'd provide a little white noise to aid my slumber. If you're planning on copying this, and I recommend you do, then don't load it up with the ingredients for cement; leave it empty or fill it with wet laundry. The photograph I took of the cement mixer was an action shot, it was in motion and my soaked onesie collection was going for a spin in the beast's mouth. Photographs should say a lot about you and I feel like this one spoke volumes about me. Specifically, I own fifteen onesies and have a functioning cement mixer at the foot of my bed. What more do you need to know? An iconic photograph.

Oh, also, I'm trying to say 'photograph' these days and not 'photo' because I'm not five years old. If you're an adult and you still say 'photo' then you need to take a long hard look at yourself (or a long hard look at a photograph of yourself). Every time I hear a grown-up saying 'photo' I have to fight the urge to yell 'graph' and, full disclosure, I don't always win that fight. In short, you've quit the internet now so start acting like it and say words properly.

Anyway, I began to take photos and it was – in a word – expensive as fuck. I was taking the same amount of pics as I did back in my online days, only now I was burning through five rolls of film a day minimum and having to pay every time I wanted them developed. If my breakfast looked eye-catching, that'd be half a roll gone before I'd left the house. Every James would eat up the rest of the roll thanks to the number of attempts it took to get the lighting, angle and my goddamn face just right. One would assume that a camera, big as it is, would hold more photos than an iddy-biddy mobile phone but that, of course, is inexplicably not the case. I was also beginning to miss being able to receive phone calls whenever I liked and, while I absolutely did not want to buy a camera phone, I did find myself fantasising over a phone camera.

I don't understand why no one has invented a camera that can receive phone calls yet. Surely, it's something we've all considered Dragons-Denning. The device would look like a standard photographer's camera but would have a telephone built into the side panel. This way you get the two best features of a camera phone (the camera and the phone) without the rotten, morally barren, shit-swamp of the internet being involved. You'd have the option of putting the ringer on silent, of course. In case you're photographing a gaggle of antelope or an unfaithful partner rendezvousing with their lover. You don't want to scare them away and scupper your chance at becoming wildlife photographer of the year or, even better, blissfully divorced from a scumbag.

But, seeing as phone cameras don't exist, I stuck with my phoneless camera and by the end of week one I found myself in two major binds: a) taking photographs was costing me a small fortune and b) I still didn't have a platform by which I could share my new photographs. It was all well and good being able to take photographs again but I used to be able to share them with the entire world at the drop of a hat. I don't know if you've ever been the only person to see your own photography but it feels weird, almost perverted in a way I can't fully explain. I needed to get my photographs seen by others, but how? Then it hit me, like an 18000-watt flash bulb in the

Roque de los Muchachos Observatory (don't you dare google that reference, you either get it or you don't. Be strong).

It was a Thursday and I had visited an art gallery to check out a new photography exhibition. As I made my way round the exhibition, taking Jameses every five seconds so I didn't forget my visit, a security guard approached me.

'You can't take photos in here,' he said.

'OK. First of all – grow up. This is a photography exhibition, not a photo exhibition, and you're representing the gallery. Secondly – your rule makes no sense. If you can't take photographs in a photography exhibition, then where can you take them? I'm celebrating the form!'

He then proceeded to bollock me and say 'photo' a bunch more times but I wasn't listening because I'd had an idea. I was just as much of a photographer as whoever had put this exhibition on (I forget their name, I was too busy taking photographs) – I could host my very own exhibition and charge people an entrance fee! That way I could share my photographs AND make money from them. And that's exactly what I did and recommend you do too. Here's how I done it.

Step one – hire out a room in an art gallery. If you don't think you can afford this then may I recommend doing what I did. I contacted a multi-millionaire by the name of Clancy Dellahue and asked her to help me out. Clancy Dellahue is a big fan of my comedy. I performed a rip-roaring set at a fundraiser she was hosting for anxious birds that couldn't confidently peck. After the gig, we bonded over a shared love of my stand-up and she promised that if I ever needed a favour she would be there. Contacting her to ask for the money was tricky as I didn't own a phone but I was able to visit one of the bird sanctuaries she'd built. I initially asked to speak to Clancy

but the staff refused to put me in touch as they had no way
of knowing I wasn't a troublemaker. Apparently, many people
hate Clancy Dellahue as they believe that birds who can't peck
should be left to their own devices and learn how to slurp or
such else. This left me with no choice but to return dressed as
a scarecrow and watch the birds go apeshit. The staff were livid
with me and threatened to call their boss – none other than
Clancy Dellahue. Obviously this was exactly what I wanted
so I didn't stand in their way (even though, as a scarecrow, I
did a lot of standing that day). Clancy turned up at the aviary,
ready to destroy this scarecrow chancer, but when she saw it
was me, she erupted in a gleeful fit of laughter and offered to
buy me a birdseed slushie (instant yes from me). I explained
my photography dilemma to Clancy, she more than understood
my predicament and was beyond happy to assist. The staff at
that aviary still hate me to this day.

My plan was simple. Clancy would walk into a gallery and
buy up an entire exhibition, leaving them desperately needing
to fill the space with a new load of photographs. I would then
rush in and offer to host my own exhibition, providing they
didn't charge me for the room. Clancy suggested a different
plan – to simply hire a room in a gallery directly, employing
no trickery. But I insisted we went with my plan. It failed and
we went with hers instead.

As I was setting up my photography exhibition, Clancy hung
around for a chinwag.

'Promise me you'll call on me more often from now on!'
she warbled and handed me a card with her address printed
on it. I promised that I would if I needed to but assured her
that wouldn't happen. Living offline was going to be easy and
I couldn't foresee missing anything other than photography.

'Suit yourself!' Clancy chirped, then adjusted her tiara, tapped her extremely long cigarette holder until the ash fell in a small pile on the floor and waltzed out of the gallery, sequined dress dragging for minutes behind her, a nameless pug puppy following closely. She was eighty-five years old.

Photography exhibitions

My first photography exhibition opened the following Sunday, showcasing countless images of my day-to-day life. Photographs of my meals, my own face, random dogs, odd-looking strangers on public transport and some snaps of my relatives with their faces blocked out. They personally requested to be blocked out as they had already disowned me and didn't want me taking their photographs in the first place but no photograph album is complete without some family pics so I'd gatecrashed my baldy of a dad's birthday BBQ and papped away, much to everyone's chagrin. For the censorship, I bought some smiley face stickers from an arts and crafts shop and stuck them directly onto the photographs, over the heads of anyone related to me. I'd seen people do this online with emojis when they didn't want the public to learn the identities of their ugly children.

I asked all visitors to *Through An Average Guy's Eyes* to give a clear, strong and literal thumbs up to any photos that appealed to them and provided chalkboards underneath the photos for any comments they had. The comments usually started out in a good place but inevitably the visitors always ended up arguing amongst themselves, usually about various forms of bigotry, a subject not deliberately raised in my photography but I let everyone have at it, all the same.

I was loving having my photographs seen by so many people again but I found myself wanting to see some of *their* photographs in return. So, in addition to my own photography exhibitions, I began hosting exhibitions for other people. Namely anyone who had already viewed my work, enabling me to get a good look at *their* selfies and dinners for once. Within just a few weeks I went from hiring a room in a gallery to hiring the entire gallery (thank you, Clancy Dellahue). Every room belonged to a different photographer and the photographs were updated on a daily basis.

Everyone brought their A-game but, naturally, I had one or two favourites. Since leaving social media, I'd missed laughing at photographs taken by weirdos I barely knew, so Reuben Farmsworth had come along at just the right time.

Where to start with Reuben? Reuben is obsessed with vintage Munch Bunch yoghurt pots and has a collection of over seven hundred which he photographs routinely. He's basically nuts. I thought I was Reuben's only fan but we had the people from the Turner Prize come to look at his exhibition the other day and they seemed impressed by the 'authentic voice' that comes across in his work (yeah, authentic *weird* voice!). Fingers crossed he makes the shortlist because more people could do with a laugh, especially during the Turner Prize exhibition, which is usually a pretentious snooze-fest for turbo-twerps.

My favourite exhibition at Real Lives Really Photographed (the name I gave to the entire gallery) belonged to a lady named Mrs Eves who exclusively exhibited photographs of her gormless dog, Gerard. Back in my online days, I used to scroll through images of other people's dogs and cats for hours. I found them extremely comforting and, since getting off the grid, I had been experiencing withdrawal. In short, I needed to see photos of strangers' pets, stat. Before hosting the exhibitions, I was on a very slippery path. I had been helping myself to any 'MISSING PET' posters around town just so I could look at the pictures. I did start to feel bad after a while and decided to make it up to all the owners by finding every single pet I'd taken a poster of – all thirty-seven of them. Luckily, this only took three days as the animals had all met each other during their time on the streets and formed an animal gang. I rounded the corner into an alleyway one afternoon and found fifteen dogs, twelve cats, five hamsters, three guinea pigs, a budgie and a tortoise all asleep in a big pile next to the bins of a Chinese takeaway. I looked like a total legend when I phoned the owners and reunited them with their best friends, refusing to accept the reward money and asking instead to be paid in pet photographs. I later learnt that during their time together, the animal gang had many adventures: solving three crimes, saving the lives of seventeen children and meeting the Clintons (Billary, respectively). One of the owners turned out to be a screenwriter and I can reveal that *Animal Gang* is coming to an online streaming platform near you very soon. The online aspect of it does mean I'm unable to watch but it's all good – I met the animal gang in real life and that's better than any fake TV show. Also, congratulations to Big Tom Davies, who I believe has been cast in the role of the local dogcatcher that gets outsmarted by the animal gang every week, a role I auditioned for but didn't get despite the fact I literally tracked the animal gang down in real life and found them. Congratulations, Tom.

Real Lives Really Photographed has been a roaring success. It felt incredible to have my photography seen by others and immerse myself in their honest, sometimes brutal feedback. I have since booked several week-long residencies at various art galleries and am now at the point where I'm never not hosting a photography exhibition. I also hire out local cinemas to screen self-filmed videos of various concerts I've been to, the crowning jewel of which is Paul McCartney at the O2. I had brought along a camcorder to capture the live experience – it was totally sold out and I wanted to show anyone not lucky enough to secure a ticket exactly what it was like to be there. For this reason, the tickets to the screening of my independent film cost the same as the tickets to see McCartney at the O2. It didn't seem fair that they should pay less than I did for exactly the same thing.

Project Offline

The photography exhibition turned out to be a great way of replicating the online experience while remaining firmly offline and it gave me an idea. When you quit something, you have to replace it with something else. That's Quitting 101. I needed to find my social media vape-stick – something that felt similar even if it made me look stupider.

There were a lot of bases to cover. I made a list of everything social media used to contribute to my life and vowed to find a way of recreating them in my new offline life. I called it . . . Project Offline.

Some things were easy to replicate providing I was willing to swallow a little pride. I became one of those people who said 'hashtag' out loud for example. At first it felt a little icky but it quickly became second nature and now I say 'hashtag James Acaster', 'hashtag *Pulp Fiction*', 'hashtag shepherd's pie', 'hashtag Watergate', 'hashtag whoops', 'hashtag lightbulb challenge' and a whole host of awful hashtags without even thinking about how cringe it objectively is. Hashtag cringe. Hashtag objectively cringe. Hashtag project offline. Not all aspects of social media would prove as easy to transfer over into my three-dimensional life but, before we go on, I want to remind you – I did succeed. I now live an offline life and I achieved it without losing any of my online privileges. If you want the same thing, all you have to do is copy my actions, beat for beat. Starting with the hashtag thing. Hashtag just copy James. Hashtag JCJ. Hashtag do it.

Project Offline began with a long to-do list but I was excited to work my way down it and elevate my entire existence. Top of my list was the thing I was most concerned about so I started there. Bullet point number one simply read: 'Friends'.

Friends

I know you feel scared. You think that if you delete all your social media accounts you will become unimportant and cease to matter. Well, I'm here to tell you – that is true.

As soon as you leave these sacred websites people will, pretty rapidly, stop giving a shit about you and, in most cases, forget you ever existed. But ask yourself this – why is that a bad thing?

When I came off social media, I walked the Earth completely anonymous for the first time since birth. No one tried to get in touch, I got blanked by close friends on a regular basis, I became the real-life Invisible Man. This meant I could do whatever I wanted, whenever I wanted, without anyone ever noticing. If they *did* notice, then I could always use my Invisible Man powers to fly mega-fast around the Earth in the wrong direction until everyone went back in time and forgot they ever laid eyes on me. That's why Invisible Man is number one.

You might think that having the entire world forget who I am has resulted in me being way more lonely than I'm currently letting on but that couldn't be further from the truth, I swear on my life. Sure, I've lost all my online friends (AKA *all my friends*) but I've retained every acquaintance I had *before* the Age of the Internet. This did mean that when I left social media I found myself with a friendship group of only four (including me) but that's A-OK because, as I like to say, friendship is about quality and not quantity (that's an Acaster Original, please credit me any time you relay this saying to others, as opposed to stealing it and passing it off as your own). I've already told you about Demetri the road worker and my millionaire benefactor Clancy Dellahue but I've not yet introduced you to my number one very best friend in the whole wide world. A man who needs no introduction. Unless you don't know who he is, which you don't, so I'm going to give you the entire backstory to our friendship right now.

Jason McKenzie

My best friend these days is someone I've known since primary school and have always kept in contact with via the medium of letter writing. No emails, no DMs, just physical pen-to-pad handwritten correspondence. When I was a seven-year-old, attending school in Kettering, everyone in my class was assigned a pen pal. The pen pal would be a pupil from St Arnold's Elementary, an institution far, far away in the City of London. I remember the lesson during which our pen pals were unveiled, the classroom was abuzz with anticipation – who would get the coolest pen pal and who would get saddled with a dud? Well, I'm pleased to announce that I fell into the former category because I was assigned a fellow by the name of Jason McKenzie. Jason McKenzie was easily the most intelligent of all the pen pals, he possessed a maturity the others lacked and his grammar was second to none. Jason McKenzie also happened to be a primary school teacher and was thirty-seven years old. There were thirty-five children in our class but the St Arnold's class only contained thirty-four corresponding children. So one kid from our lot got paired up with the St Arnold's teach. I didn't care that the rest of my class got chosen by the students of St Arnold's and I didn't. Although upon reflection it was weird that my teacher, Mrs Frostly, told me as much. She could've just lied and said the pen pals were assigned randomly but instead revealed that all of the St Arnold's lot had a choice and none of them chose me. But, in her defence, I did ask her to 'give it to me straight'. Frostly confirmed that the St Arnold's class were presented with our photographs and profiles (candidly written by Frostly herself) and mine was ultimately the least appealing of the bunch. Cop a load of this shit:

Pupil's Name: Acaster, James William Jericho
Interests: health and safety, his own step count, the life and times of Beatrix Potter
Favourite Film: March of the Penguins 1
Skills: poi, yodelling, can recite biblical parables by heart
Weaknesses: poor balance, fear of cartoons, prone to rashes
Catchphrase: 'Howdy partners, let's get learnin''

My first instinct was to be angry at Frostly for making me sound like a dud but then I realised she was in the saddest position of all – Mrs Frostly was now the *only* person in this equation not to have a pen pal. Poor Frostly was sure to feel left out every time the school post arrived but that's what you get for smearing the reputation of the coolest kid in class.

Any residual feelings of ill will I had towards Frostly were promptly quashed when I received my very first letter from Jason McKenzie. Lemme tell ya: this guy can write prose. Jason McKenzie was a university graduate and an adult and therefore an excellent penman. The words really leapt off the page, he could tell an anecdote with the best of them and his nose for satire was second to none. This meant I had to up my game as I knew he'd be reading my replies with a critical eye and, although he would never directly slag me off, I feared he would curse me in private if I sent even the slightest whiff of literary dog mess. It was this overwhelming, visceral fear of inadequacy that drove me to become a top-tier letter writer and the distinctive author I am today (exhibit A – this book). The stories I regaled him with were your standard childhood japes but the skill, as any raconteur knows, was in the telling. I messed around with the form a lot in those early days, doing away with linear narratives and allowing myself to jump back and forth along the timeline, as and when the mood struck me. When I told the story of Benjamin Priestly stepping in a puddle I started at the end and ended at the beginning, essentially cheating a happy ending. One letter, detailing the time my paddling grandfather got followed for half an hour by a lone jellyfish, was told from multiple perspectives: my grandad, the jellyfish, the sea and the lifeguard who eventually saved his life by pissing on the jellyfish until it fizzed and melted. The best reaction I ever got from McKenzie was when, aged nine, I wrote him a letter that ended with a twist (I'd been dead the whole time). He did not see it coming, despite the fact that when one reread the letter, it seemed so obvious from the beginning. As you can imagine, by the end of primary school I could write the hell out of a pen pal letter. I had gotten so good, in fact, that Jason McKenzie and I continued to stay in touch long after primary school was over – something that cannot be said for my fellow classmates and their so-called 'pals'.

It's not as weird as it sounds, by the way. When I graduated primary school and got promoted to secondary school, I simply informed my new form tutor that I would be retaining my pen pal from primary school and asked for him to be added to my own personal syllabus. This kept everything above board for the next six years, at the end of which I was officially a grown-up, free to write letters to whomever I wanted – and I wanted to write letters to Jason McKenzie. By this point we had transcended pen 'pal' status and were pen companions (or 'comPENions' as Jason McKenzie once jested in a particularly witty slab of correspondence). We had in-jokes that went back to pre-pubescence (for one of us, anyway, and the other doesn't love being reminded of the fact) and we still got on like a house on fire. A house that had been on fire for ten years without the fire brigade being able to put it out. A roaring fire that had long gutted the inside of the building and yet the basic structure of the house remained standing, probably held up by loyalty, friendship and laughs. I continued writing to Jason McKenzie throughout my twenties and he gave me great advice in the early stages of my comedy career. As a teacher, he really knew how to hold a crowd's attention and shake the pre-gig jitters: 'Don't imagine they're naked, imagine they're dead and nothing you do matters.' Invaluable. The advice went both ways, of course. In return, I counselled him through an ugly divorce (reader, he was too good for her). Best ComPENion ever.

I actually only stopped writing letters to Jason McKenzie as recently as 2020. By then I was thirty-five, but don't worry, we didn't fall out or anything, quite the opposite – we became housemates. I had lived in London since I was eighteen years old, having bought the detached house I'd intended to transform into a castle. McKenzie and I had always talked about meeting for the first time but our diaries never quite synced up until March 2020. He travelled across London to pay me a visit and we had the greatest time. It was as if our letters had come to life and were hanging out for the day. We challenged a group of old men to a game of tag-team bowls and destroyed them, we ate our body weight in babka and got our photo on the wall of my local Babkery, we released sky lanterns outside Buckingham Palace and sang karaoke in my back garden until my neighbours begged us to stop so their fussy baby could get to sleep. It was the best day.

Jason McKenzie was hugely impressed when I told him I'd quit social media and became inspired to do the same. This did lead to a rather awkward moment when I had to ask Demetri for a little more tar, causing my two friends to meet for the first time. It's always tricky when you mix friendship groups and showing up on Demetri's doorstep asking to borrow a bucket of warm tar for Jason McKenzie was no exception. Demetri clearly felt threatened by this wizened old scholar who'd known me for decades and Jason McKenzie was obviously wary of this hip new cat with all the tar hook-ups. I knew I had to get them to bond somehow so I thought fast.

'Hey! Why don't you paint over your laptop and phone with tar too, Demetri? We can all be one big gang!'

There was a beat, during which I thought I'd hoofed the whole thing over the crossbar, before Demetri softly said, 'That's the single most bodacious idea I have ever heard.'

The golden trio

One group hug and several high fives later, the two of them had caked their respective devices in tar and we'd hopped on the fast train to Rhyll. The train was totally empty and we had an entire carriage to ourselves. We spent the whole journey singing songs about friendship and the inevitable fall of modern technology.

I'll admit, I was a tad concerned that I'd receive more abuse from the bullies of Rhyll but, on this particular afternoon, it was a ghost town. We walked from the train station to Fill 'Em Up, Rhyll 'Em Up without encountering a single human soul. The FEUREU staff even managed to keep their distance from us, giving us a wide berth as we waltzed in and made our way up to my storage unit. Demetri and Jason McKenzie chucked their devices into the unit without a second thought. The tarred goods clattered on top of mine and they bid them good riddance. The only slight hiccup came when I gazed down and laid eyes on my phone and laptop for the first time since their initial deposit. I couldn't quite handle the sudden temptation. It occurred to me, in that moment, that I could retrieve my belongings if I so pleased. They were right there and there was nothing stopping me. This idle thought soon developed into a ferocious need and, without knowing how I got there, I found myself lunging at the devices I once held dear. Demetri and Jason McKenzie leapt into action, dragging me away from the unit before I could lay a finger on anything, pinning me against the far wall as I squirmed like crazy.

'I just want to touch them again, that's all,' I said like a pathetic liar. 'No funny business.'

'Come on, friend,' said McKenzie in a soothing voice, 'let's just hop on the train back to the Big Smoke. We'll be walking that drawbridge in no time.'

I wriggled some more.

'Please, James,' begged Demetri. 'We're in this together now. Our devices are all tarred up in a beautiful, dank, dark storage unit. I cut my finger open while smashing my camera lens on a tin opener; it was frightening and erotic at the same time. We can't lose this already.'

I broke down in tears and fell into Jason McKenzie's arms, sobbing like a scared little baba. My two friends carried me as I staggered through the desolate town, back to the empty station and onto the silent train home. The relief I felt when we arrived at my house was unreal. My friends laid me down on my bed and made me a hot mug of half-cocoa, half-marsh-mallows. We put our feet up and switched on the wireless just in time for *Chuck Pewsley's Skiffle Hour*. As the sweet sounds of washboards and slide whistles filled the room, Jason McKenzie opened that day's newspaper to learn that yesterday, a national lockdown had been announced due to a global pandemic.

Luckily, Jason McKenzie had brought an overnight bag with him so immediately called dibs on the kitchen futon. This made me feel sorry for Demetri so I offered him my personal bed which he accepted without a second thought. However, the joke was on both those guys because I knew the softest surface in my entire flat was my extra fluffy bath mat, which I slept on most nights anyway. We each drifted off to the Land of Nod, one in a bed, one on a futon and one on a very nice bath mat, and, just like that, it was official – the three of us were ULDBs (Ultimate Lock Down Buddies).

Achievement and greatness

Fast forward to 19 July 2021. Jason McKenzie, Demetri and I had been locked down together for sixteen months. Not only that, we had been locked down together *without the internet* for sixteen months. In other words, at no point during the pandemic did we know what the hell was going on. We only knew about 'Freedom Day' because my postman had bellowed, 'HAPPY FREEDOM DAY!' at the top of his lungs from the street one morning. The three of us looked out of the slits in the castle walls to see him, totally nude, urinating into our moat and flipping us the bird. We concluded the world must be opening up again because he wasn't wearing a face mask.

Finishing the castle had become our lockdown project and we'd done a bloody good job of it. Sure, the moat stank and an aggressive family of gulls had claimed one of the turrets as their own but, all in all, this was a huge achievement. An achievement we never would've pulled off had the three of us been sitting around, glued to our phones every second of the day. The pandemic had completely removed the temptation of travelling to Rhyll to retrieve our devices because doing such a thing had become illegal. Sure, we got the shakes and sweats for the first couple of months but we pushed through and, by August, were clear-headed and daisy-fresh. We had drawn up the plans for the castle back in July 2020 and Demetri had used his contacts in construction to procure the appropriate kit. We worked on Castle Anti-Net (the name of the castle) day and night. Anti-Net was a pun on 'Internet'. Anti means against. So the castle was against the internet. It works.

Castle Anti-Net. Anti-Internet.

It's not shit.

We worked on Castle Anti-Net round the clock, never once getting distracted by a single website, and as a result I still, to this day, know virtually nothing about the Covid-19 pandemic. I'm aware a lot of important stuff happened, and I intend to catch up eventually, but back when everything was kicking off, I was mainly obsessed with building a castle. Even Jason McKenzie, who usually reads the newspaper religiously, didn't have time to swot up because he'd got heavily into designing the castle gift shop. He stocked that baby up wonderfully: stationery, T-shirts, caps and let's not forget, chopping boards. Our suppliers were giving away the chopping boards as part of a deal – if you ordered upwards of ten fish bowls then they threw in the chopping boards half price – and Jason McKenzie knows a good deal when he sees one. Every item featured the Castle Anti-Net official logo – three soldiers in a castle, pouring a cauldron of hot tar from the highest turret onto a giant mobile phone. The mobile was attempting to attack the castle, that was the idea. In the actual olden days, soldiers would pour hot oil onto attackers but we thought tar worked better due to our own personal history with mobile phones. Not that anyone can tell the difference between tar and oil in a drawing but whatever. Anyway, we had to explain the logo to every single person who bought an item from our gift shop. The only detail that never got questioned on the logo was the violence. Because violence quickly became associated with our castle thanks to the areas we opened up to the public. All of which were objectively violent. This was a) the last thing we wanted and b) Demetri's fault.

The lockdowns affected everyone in different ways and Demetri certainly emerged from them way kookier than he was before. To put it lightly. As a road worker, Demetri was already highly skilled when it came to constructing things. This is why, during a global pandemic, this man built the best castle dungeon I've ever seen. It was a London/Edinburgh type dungeon, rather than a fully functioning, fit-for-purpose dungeon. A tourist attraction of sorts, to give the local kids a laugh once things had opened up again. Demetri dipped a load of mannequins in corn syrup and arranged them in awful positions like they were being viciously tortured, chopping some of them up and scattering their body parts round the dank rooms within the dingy basement. It was pretty grim, the mannequins looked disturbing, and Demetri didn't tell us he was working on the dungeon until we discovered it by accident. When questioned, he did assure us that we were correct in assuming it was 'a London/ Edinburgh type dungeon, rather than a fully functioning, fit-for-purpose dungeon', though. He was very keen that we stick to that assumption. So we did, because it felt safer.

In case you're wondering – Clancy Dellahue paid for the whole castle. We wrote her letters any time we needed funding and she was more than happy to assist because she was bored out of her mind during lockdown and thought it was hilarious that we were building a castle. God bless Clancy Dellahue and all her money.

Spending the pandemic in a castle was fantastic. We couldn't have been more isolated. We lowered the drawbridge for deliveries only, meaning anyone who wanted to infect us with the coronavirus was going to have to swim across a moat first. A moat with an electric eel in, may I add. In medieval times they would sometimes have sharks in their moats. I think. I'm not sure, we were unable to google anything or get to a library during the pando. But we *were* able to pester one C Dellahue into buying us an electric eel. She sent one of her best boys round to plop it in the moat and it's been doing laps of the castle ever since. The eel's name is Enid, she's a rescue and at night-time she puts on quite the light show. Enid has only had to zap one person so far and that person was Tom from MySpace. Apparently restraining orders mean nothing to the guy and he tried to infiltrate Castle Anti-Net in order to guilt me into rejoining MySpace again. This was at 3 a.m. and I guess he couldn't see the moat in the dark so splashed on in, limbs flailing. What he definitely *could* see in the dark, though, was Enid flying towards him like a neon sock possessed. She zapped him good, right in the belly button, and he lit up like the Fourth of July. We watched Tom clamber out of the moat after the zapping and he looked frazzled, hair standing on end and covered in soot. Jason McKenzie yelled, 'Friend request denied!' from the West Tower and we all had a ruddy good laugh as Tom sizzled on the pavement. Demetri said he saw someone cook an egg on him but we think he made that up.

Freedom Day was weird for us. The whole thing sounded stupid (both as a name and as an idea) but it was also weird in a way that was specific to our situation. When we'd collectively decided to come offline we'd felt euphoric but, deep down, we were terrified of relapsing. Then the pandemic came along and put our lives on pause. This turned out to be a massive positive for us as it meant we didn't notice the absence of the World Wide Web due to the World Wide *World* grinding to a standstill. Freedom Day changed all that. 'Freedom' meant choice. For the first time in a long time, we could choose to go back to our old ways. We could get our phones out of storage, scrape off the tar and rejoin the Borg OR we could do what we set out to and live a rich *offline* life. I could feel Jaym Baecaster stirring deep within my loins. I still needed to replace the things the internet had once given me with real tangible things, out in the real world. Otherwise, I would be on a train to Rhyll faster than a train to Rhyll. So I decided to pick up Project Offline where I'd left off: 'Friends' – or, more specifically – 'New Friends'.

New Friends

The internet had enabled me to make new friends whenever I so pleased. Jason McKenzie, Clancy Dellahue and Demetri (surname unknown) were all tremendous, as people and as compatriots, but I definitely had more than three friends at the peak of my Facebook days. The question was: how the hell did I used to make friends before the internet? I pondered this question for a long, long time, wracking the corridors of my mind for the answer, and when I hit upon it, I didn't waste a second. I leapt out of bed, lowered the drawbridge and marched into town, determined to do what needed to be done. In short, I joined the Scouts.

Little tip for you: if you're in your thirties, you can still join the Scouts so long as you can provide a good argument for why the troop should accept you (along with a recent and valid CRB check). I put it to the Scoutmasters that, while I had attended Scouts as a teen, I'd hardly achieved any of the sacred badges up for grabs. Bottom line, I was too busy wisecracking with my pals to earn a lil' stitch. Fast forward to 2021, and I was essentially returning to the movement in order to retake my exams and get my qualifications (à la Billy Madison). The Scoutmasters found my attitude towards badges 'refreshing' and agreed to grant me a second chance. However, as you and

I know, the only badge I was actually after was the 'friendship badge'. Because I was there to make friends. But also because the friendship badge was an actual badge. You could achieve the actual friendship badge simply by bringing a non-Scouting friend to a Scout meeting. No prizes for guessing which pal I had in mind but I didn't want to cross my worlds over just yet so I kept Jason McKenzie in the back pocket and focussed on making friends with some ten to fourteen year olds.

I'm pleased to report that when it comes to making friends the Scouts still reigns supreme. As soon as I joined the troop, I was assigned a patrol. Said patrol consisted of myself and five other Scouts – Adam (patrol leader), Isaac, Sonny, Chris and Mimi. Mimi was a girl and that was fair enough. Girls had been allowed in the Scouts towards the tail end of my original Scouting run so I knew encountering one would be a possibility and I'm pleased to report that Mimi was a credit to her neckerchief and would've made Baden Powell proud (had he not probably hated women). And so it was that Isaac, Mimi and Chris became my first new friends since going offline. Three out of five ain't bad. Sonny was too busy earning badges to make friends and Adam was too busy being a killjoy who sucks. I'd rather not focus on Adam too much. I'd prefer to fill these pages with tales of the Tangfastic Four (a name we came up with due to our mutual love of fizzy sweets and the Marvel Cinematic Universe) but suffice to say Adam was a dick. Not Ernie Freedman levels of dickness but still pretty bad. Before I joined the crew, the Tangfastic Four were known as the Fortnite Three, after a computer game they all raved about and have since taught me the dance moves to. From the moment my first Scout meeting began, it was clear that they were the cools. I wanted in, but in order to make it, I'd have to prove I was a laugh. Challenge accepted. Within five minutes, I'd delivered a savage impersonation of a little character by the name of Gareth and been fully inducted into the gang. Gareth was the Scoutmaster. He spat when he talked, he had bad hair, a bum chin, and was a mimic's dream. Don't let his title fool you, though. Despite being an adult and the master of the entire Scout troop, Gareth was still nine years my junior. This meant that I sort of leapfrogged him when it came to winning the respect of my fellow Scouts and I definitely showed him mercy by not organising what would've been a very easy mutiny. My patrol leader and all-round square, Adam, told me off for doing an impression of Gareth, saying it was 'pathetic' and 'if it was a good impression you wouldn't need to say "My name's Gareth" over and over'. When Adam was delivering this bollocking, a panic swept over me – had I lost the ability to make friends? Would everyone just think I was 'pathetic' now? If the patrol leader didn't think I was cool then surely the rest of the patrol would follow suit, right? Wrong, actually. Chris soon extended his fist to me, not in a violent way but in a way that indicated respect. I bumped his fist with my own balled-up hand and that seemed to inspire nods from Mimi and Isaac, indicating even more respect and admiration. Sonny, however, was refusing to make eye contact because he was intently listening to whatever Gareth was waffling on about. Poor Sonny never missed a word that old sap said. I don't think I need to point out the irony here – out of all the Scouts in that Scout troop, Sonny was the one who would've appreciated my impersonation the most but he was too busy watching the man himself to even glimpse it. Another thing that played into my hands when it came to making fun of Gareth was that none of my fellow Scouts had heard the expression 'Say it, don't spray it' before, so I was able to pass it off as my own and they thought I was a genius.

From that day forth, Isaac, Mimi, me and Chris were best friends and everybody knew it (I know grammatically speaking that should read 'Isaac, Mimi, Chris and I' but Chris is definitely bottom of the pile status-wise and I can't bring myself to plop my name *after* his in a list just because it's proper English). We were the loudest Scouts in that Scout troop, always getting told to pipe down by Gareth (or 'The Sprinkler' as we now called him), who would then tell Adam to control his patrol, causing Adam to yell at us out of his weirdly small mouth (once you noticed how small his mouth was, it was impossible to unsee it). The Tangfastic Four got on super well even though we all went to different schools. Isaac went to a Christian school, Mimi went to a business academy, Chris went to the roughest school in town, and I was thirty-six. It felt good to be making actual, real-life friends again. To be interacting like legends, laughing together and telling each other hysterical stories. I felt sorry for the rest of the world with their unfulfilling online friendships; they would never know how much fun they could be having for only £78 (£55 for the full Scout uniform plus the CRB check costs £23 and takes up to four weeks to process).

Sadly, it wasn't long before my patrol leader and all-round dweeb, Adam, informed Gareth that the Tangfastic Four were driving him crazy and delivered a hefty ultimatum – if I didn't leave then he would have to take a sabbatical from the Boy Scouts.

Adam began his sabbatical the following day and from what I hear, it's been great for him. However, Adam's sabbatical hasn't reflected well on the Scout troop as a whole. A fourteen-year-old boy being forced to take a stress-induced leave of absence due to the antics of a man in his thirties who had unprecedentedly been allowed to join the troop due to his mild celebrity status (assistant troop leader Brian was a fan) proved hard to square with some of the less fun mums and dads. But we weathered the storm and I'm pleased to announce that I have since earned my 'dealing with the local press' badge. I've also been made a Patrol Leader since 'a certain someone' couldn't handle the pressure and quit for good. As if this wasn't good news enough, Sonny decided to stop being a dweeb and join the Tangfastic Four AND Gareth caved in and allowed Jason McKenzie to also join the troop (he already had a pristine CRB from his teaching days). The Tangfastic Four was now the Tangfastic Six AKA we were cooler than ever and I achieved it all without being on any social media sites whatsoever. Check the scoreboard, folks, because it's James Acaster 1, Internet 0.

Naturally, Jason McKenzie and I asked the Tangfastic Six if they cared to welcome Demetri into the fold and, out of this one tiny request, the Tangfastic Crew was born. We couldn't be bothered to keep changing the number in the name, so took a vote and went with 'crew' (it beat 'gang', 'posse' and 'bunch'). The castle became our clubhouse, Enid the eel became our mascot and the photography exhibitions earned us a little extra coin (the castle gift shop was making diddly squat). Since three of us had already adopted the offline lifestyle, we decided to make the Tangfastic Crew an offline affair. This meant Isaac, Mimi, Chris and Sonny had to go through something of an induction ceremony. They all painted over their devices with tar (Demetri snuck another bucket out of work) and we all trained it down to Rhyll to chuck them in storage. Once again, I frantically tried to retrieve my belongings from the storage unit but the less said about that the better. Thankfully, my crew dragged me out hooting and hollering and we made it back to the castle without any of us glancing at a single phone screen. What a tremendous crew. We asked Clancy Dellahue if she wanted to join but she said no.

How do I keep tabs on everyone I went to school with?

Making new friends was proving easy as peach pie but what of my old friends? And I don't just mean the friends who'd cut me out of their lives due to my extreme-to-the-point-of-irresponsible Facebook-leaving antics. I'm talking old, old, dusty, ancient, mummified friends – people I'd long lost touch with, people I went to school with and, thanks to social media, people I'd easily kept tabs on over the years. I used to love knowing what all of my ex-classmates were up to and peeping on their lives had become a cherished part of my daily routine, but now I'd locked myself out of the observation bubble and swallowed the key. Also, to continue the metaphor, it didn't look like I'd be passing the key any time soon as I'd painted over my anus with tar. I didn't know what to do so I asked the Tangfastic Crew. As the first member to quit social media, I had become the leader by default, but I still consulted them before making any big decisions. Mimi thought the answer was obvious and couldn't believe I hadn't thought of it already.

'There's only one valid option here, PLS. You need to organise a class reunion.'

I couldn't have agreed with her more. By the way, PLS stands for Patrol Leader Supreme.

First things first, I needed a venue. My old secondary school seemed like the obvious choice so I headed on over to see if I couldn't bag the activity hall for a night.

Sidenote: during my schooldays, I'd never questioned the name 'activity hall' but as an adult it now sounded ridiculous. I used to hear those words every single day and not give them a second thought but now here I was, a thirty-six-year-old man, asking the new head of my old school if the 'activity hall' was available and I felt like a moron for having the gall to say 'activity hall' like it didn't make me sound like a massive baby. Activity hall. A hall for activities. What goes on in that hall? Activities. Any specific activities? No, just any and all activities. Every single activity in the world? Yes, if you've got an activity then this is the hall for it. REALLY?! Put some effort in, lads.

It might sound obvious but, bottom line, every hall is an activity hall. Name me a hall where no activities take place and I'll shut up but I just feel like the word 'activity' is a little redundant when it comes to naming a hall. Most *things* are activities. Tossing the caber is an activity, cutting your toenails is an activity, anything you have ever done is unarguably an activity. So as soon as you set foot in any hall (setting foot is an activity) it becomes an activity hall. Every dancehall is an activity hall, the Royal Albert Hall is an activity hall, even the actor Michael C. Hall is an activity Hall as he's always got an activity or two on the go at any given time. The only time a hall is not an activity hall is when it's empty and no activities are taking place within it. I now regret bringing up Michael C. Hall because it means we have to figure out what entails an empty Michael C. Hall and I guess it's him being dead but, in the name of science, this still bolsters my argument so I'm keeping it in. My point is, an activity hall has no greater claim to the name activity hall than any of the aforementioned halls,

Michael C. included, because it's *not* a hall of activity 24/7 (literally). If there was an activity taking place in an activity hall *at all times* would I cool my jets and let the name slide? Absolutely. But in order for that to happen a system would have to be introduced whereby, at the end of each day, the last person out of the hall has to release a frog into the room before locking up. Frogs famously can't stop hopping so 'activity' status would be sustained throughout the night. Obviously, the next people to enter the activity hall will have to catch the frog before beginning their own activities, otherwise it's likely to get in the way, but catching a frog is also an activity so it's win-win. However, let's face facts, if the frog system is introduced, it's only a matter of time before activity halls assume the name 'frog rooms'. The fact that there's always a frog hopping around in them is way more notable than a bunch of nondescript activities, so the name 'activity hall' will get thrown out the window, 'frog rooms' will become the new normal and we're back to square one.

While we're here, 'hall' feels a little grand as well. Don't get it twisted, 'hall' is certainly pulling its weight more than 'activity' is, the room is echoey, I'll give it that, and I'm pretty sure that's the only criteria required for a hall. Once a room achieves echoey status, you have to give in and call it a hall, and if it's echoey in a long and narrow way then you have to admit it's a hallway. It's common knowledge that a hallway is only called a hallway due to the acoustics being similar to that of a hall. Although I would argue that, these days, corridors are far more echoey than hallways. I know your instinct is to argue this point but you know I'm right for so many reasons. You can have a carpeted hallway, for example, but I couldn't even begin to picture a carpeted corridor. Carpet deadens any echo, plain fact. In a corridor you can always hear the clip-clop of footsteps bouncing off the walls – it's how you know you're in a corridor. If I want some peace and quiet, I'll take a stroll down a hallway where clip-clopping may as well be outlawed. Put it this way – I've never been snuck up on in a corridor but I've been jumped in a hallway more times than I care to remember.

So, yes, it's a hall and, yes, activities take place there and I appreciate that the activities are miscellaneous in nature and tough to pin down, but perhaps if you just added the word 'miscellaneous' then the name would finally make sense. Miscellaneous Activity Hall. It doesn't trip off the tongue but it's a fairer description of the room you're walking into and if we can't give people a decent heads-up in regards to the space they're about to find themselves slap bang in the middle of then what have we become as a society? Anyway, the headteacher disagreed with me and said they wouldn't be changing the names of any rooms in the school any time soon so I thanked her for her time and bid her good day.

It wasn't until I was back in the car park that I remembered about the reunion. I jogged back into the school reception and asked if the head was still free. She wasn't and would not be again for another two hours. So I sat and I waited and used my time to draft up some alternative names for 'activity hall' that were catchier than 'Miscellaneous Activity Hall'. In the end I settled on Versatility Chamber. To my surprise, the headteacher did a complete 180 and absolutely loved this. So much so that she said I could hire the Versatility Chamber for free as a thank you. Sometimes people surprise you.

While I was there, I popped in on a couple of my old teachers to see how they were doing/to see how thrilled they were to see me, but their reaction was a little muted for my tastes and I left feeling like an absolute sack of shit. I'd secured the venue, though. Now all I had to do was contact everyone I went to school with, without using the internet.

Invitations and how to send them

The invitation process was a slog but, frankly, I loved it. It felt good to reacquaint myself not only with my classmates but with another old friend, commonly known as Mr P. Book. The P stands for phone. The phone book.

The weight of the phone book alone took me back. As soon as I picked it up, I realised that everything I'd held in my hands over the last two decades had either been lighter or heavier than a phone book. Nothing had been the exact same weight. As my fingers wrapped around its girth, I could feel the heft of the lives contained therein. I became convinced that if this book lost or gained a contact, the weight would shift and I'd be able to sense it. I stood, with my eyes closed, holding that phone book in my hallway for a good ten minutes before Jason McKenzie jumped me for a joke and snapped me out of it.

I wondered if reconnecting with my ex-classmates would feel the same as reconnecting with this phone book. Not in terms of weight, obviously. I was sure none of my classmates would weigh the same as when they were twelve. But would we slip back into old friendships the way I had with this gorgeous telephone directory? I certainly hoped not as I was mainly organising the reunion to see how tragic everyone else had become. I wanted to feel better about my own life, that was the whole point. Nothing boosts the old ego like witnessing the pathetic existence of others. It gives me the strength required to pursue my own mediocrity.

The way I wanted to feel at the reunion more closely resembled how I felt when reacquainting myself with yet another old friend – Mr P. Box. Yes, the P does stand for phone again.

I had no way of contacting my old classmates thanks to painting over my mobile phone with tar and forgetting to get a landline installed when building a castle. I grabbed a hiking sock full of loose change, headed down to the dilapidated phone box in the town centre and, woah mama, it was looking rough. A smashed window, sexual graffiti on every surface, flyers for naked ladies and someone had definitely had at least one unhealthy piss in it. Now this is what I wanted from my school chums at the reunion. I wanted to walk away from each classmate having heard a sad story and gained a sense of superiority. I didn't want to rekindle old flames, I wanted to make sure everyone else's flames had been thoroughly pissed on and then go home. This is how I'd spent my time online and I'd be damned if I was going to stop now just because I'd locked up all my devices in Rhyll and dug a moat around my own house.

The big reunion

Thanks to Monsieurs Book and Box, I managed to reach everybody. The night of the reunion, I stood by the door and watched as older versions of my ex-classmates waltzed into the Versatility Chamber, regarding each other with suppressed amusement. No one vocalised it but it was clear we were all loving how bad everyone looked and how stupid our plus-ones appeared at first glance. It was everything I'd wanted and more. The catering company I hired, Lord Chompington's, put on an amazing spread (their Chompington sliders were second to none), the band I booked were so tight I thought I was listening to the actual Crowded House and the DJ kept everyone informed as to when their taxis arrived, something he didn't have to do but said was 'all part of the service'. I had brought Isaac along with me because, as you'll know, it's important to have someone to laugh at the new lives of your old school friends with (Isaac knew all about laughing at school friends thanks to still being in school). I'd catch up with an old desk buddy, they'd tell me something sad like how they're a life coach now or how much they enjoy collecting seashells, then I'd run over to Isaac and relay the info while describing what the person was like in school for context. Then Isaac would laugh at how sad they were and I'd know I wasn't a bad person for deriving so much pleasure from someone else's misery. Then I'd run off and do it all over again.

The only downside of the physical school reunion versus spying on the internet was that I couldn't laugh the second I received the information. I always had to walk away, doing my best to stifle a guffaw, then laugh behind a plant with Isaac. Holding it together during the conversation was sometimes very difficult. I absent-mindedly punched the air when Keith Morris went off on a rant about how 9/11 was an inside job but fortunately he thought I was enthusiastically agreeing with him. He used to be the school bully but now he'd gone mad and believed every conspiracy theory he'd ever read online – it was the jackpot to end all jackpots. I kept on teeing him up, asking him what he thought of various world events, then I'd sit back and bask in his madness. He'd lost his mind and it was giving me life. Keith became quite the draw. Word spread around the reunion and a crowd soon gathered to listen to his batshit beliefs. The bigger the crowd got, the more vocal Keith became. Keith was so wrapped up in his own loopy logic that he didn't even realise the crowd consisted exclusively of people he used to throw stationery at on a daily basis. I gave Keith my postal address and encouraged him to send me a postcard whenever he felt like getting something off his chest. He said no but it was worth it to hear his thoughts on how the Royal Mail have been monitoring us for decades.

It was also important for me to catch up with Denise Willis, my very first crush. Denise was lovely in school, nice to everyone, and by all accounts is still lovely now. I don't have feelings for her any more and I don't think she was even aware I had feelings for her back in the day. I never told her and, if she did know, she certainly never acknowledged it. It went unspoken but I thought she was the most enchanting person I'd ever met and used to gaze at her from across the classroom, mesmerised by this new feeling and wondering if it was love. Anyway, she's divorced now so that felt incredible. Serves her right for being unknowingly fancied by me twenty-three years ago and not marrying me when she had the chance. I was walking on air.

Another thing that felt absolutely brilliant at the class reunion was my own popularity. Back in school no one ever wanted to talk to me but now people were queuing up to ask me about quitting social media and how I did it. They wanted to know everything – how I'd managed to join the Scouts as an adult, how I'd recently moved in with my 59-year-old pen pal . . . it really made me appreciate how rich my life had become since logging off the 'net and diving headfirst back into the real world. Many of my ex-classmates urged me to keep in touch with them, which is perfect for me as it means I can continue to receive updates on their pitiful little worlds while gloating about my own awesome existence. Here's to the class of '01 and their sad-sack, nobody, loser lives! Cheers!

How do I spy on my exes now?

In just one evening I'd managed to harvest way more goss about my ex-classmates than I ever did in a month's worth of Facebook stalking and it reminded me – Facebook used to help me liberally spy on my exes too. Don't judge! Heartbreak is a motherfucker, we've all been through it and if you haven't, you will one day and when that day comes you'll be filled with a burning desire to round-the-clock monitor the person who just broke your heart. Once a relationship is over, it's only natural to want to know what the other person is up to: how happy they are, who they're hanging out with, if they're seeing anybody new, if they've been on any nights out, what they're having for breakfast, where they went on holiday, any new purchases they've made, do they miss you, are they still in love with you and are they dead. Time was, anyone who acted on these desires was considered a deeply disturbed individual but now, praise Jesus, social media has normalised these impulses and made it easier than ever to spy on whoever you're obsessed with.

It struck me that I currently had no idea whether any of my exes missed me or if they were even alive. This feeling didn't sit well so I booked the Versatility Chamber once more, this time for an EGOJAR. EGOJAR stands for Ex-Girlfriend Of James Acaster Reunion, not that it matters because nobody showed up. Turns out the prospect of standing in an old school hall with your ex-boyfriend and all of his ex-girlfriends doesn't appeal to anyone, ever. Without the ex-girlfriends, my EGOJAR quickly became a regular JAR and I learnt that eating an entire buffet on your own is virtually impossible. Isaac tried to help me tackle the spread but the grub on offer wasn't to his tastes. The spread mainly consisted of the favourite dishes of my ex-girlfriends and most of them existed solely on a diet of BBQ ribs and poutine. Still, props to Lord Chompington's for coming through yet again. I hate wasting good grub so I called in the rest of the Tangfastic Crew as backup and they did me proud. Between us, we slayed that buffet, although the sight of Demetri aggressively eating ribs was rather unsettling. The guy was clearly getting lost in some cannibalistic fantasies and the noises he made were bordering on sexual. But each to their own. The Tangfastic Crew spent the entire evening dancing and doing karaoke as a group and it felt good to have our first official Tangfastic Party. It'd been years since I'd been at a party where everyone was physically and mentally present – not a single person staring at their phone. In a word, the evening was electric and it reaffirmed the whole point of Project Offline but then, out of nowhere, I was hit by a sudden wave of anxiety. Now that I was off social media, how would anyone ever invite me to parties? I used to be inundated with Facebook invitations but I hadn't been invited to a single party since coming offline – that couldn't be a coincidence! You don't get invited if you're not where the invites are, that's just common sense. Oh boy, this was grave stuff. Suddenly partying felt way more important than catching up with my exes so I put the ladies on hold (sorry, ladies!) and made my social life priority numero uno. Well, I ate my body weight in cheese curds and *then* I made my social life priority numero uno.

How do I get invited to parties now?

I'm a party animal. My birth certificate says human but that is inaccurate. The rookie doctor who typed that needs to get the Tipp-Ex out, paint over 'human' and write 'party animal' in block capitals because that's the true species I belong to. That said, being a party animal, I don't much care for dorky things like certificates so, y'know, whatever – throw it in the trash for all I care, I just wanna party. Back in my online days, I'd party all day and party all night, party from dusk to dawn, party in the morning, party in the noon-time, party when the sun goes down. But once you're no longer available at the click of a button, the party invites tend to dry up.

I hadn't been invited to anything for ages: birthday parties, family gatherings (I'd been ostracised, lest we forget), weddings, funerals, soirées, get togethers, shindigs or pow-wows. The Tangfastic Crew suggested I carry on hosting my own parties but they were missing the point. Party animals don't host their own parties – that's the job of dorks. Inviting loads of people to a party is pathetic, a real act of desperation. You're basically begging everyone to be your friend. Getting *invited* to parties, on the other hand, means you're officially a top-shelf cool boy because all the pathetic dorks need you to hang out with them in order to validate their own piddly existence. The downside of parties only being organised by dorks is that dorks <u>love</u> computers (always have, always will) meaning if you don't own a computer you ain't getting invited to the latest DorkFest for Cool Guys. What a conundrum. I never wanted to so much as look at a computer ever again but I desperately needed to get back on people's guest lists. More than that, I desperately needed to be *top* of people's guest lists – and that is why I started my own catering company.

Offline Hors D'oeuvres

Offline Hors D'oeuvres is the world's first catering company specialising in every type of party ever while operating 100% offline. If you want to book Offline Hors D'oeuvres then you're going to need to give us a ring. We hang out by the old phone box every Monday between the hours of 3 and 4 p.m. Being difficult to get hold of gives the company a more exclusive feel and earns us extra cool points. If you want to book Bill Murray for a film role, you have to phone his landline, that's the only way he does business. So Offline Hors D'oeuvres was like the Bill Murray of party food. I know Bill Murray did the Garfield movie but that was just because he misunderstood the brief and thought that one of the Coen brothers was making it. Doesn't totally explain why he did the second Garfield movie but I guess once you've done one Garfield movie, the damage has been done and you may as well bang out another for the cash. The point is, Offline Hors D'oeuvres was like Bill Murray had he not done the Garfield movies.

I'll address this right now – yes, written down, the name Offline Hors D'oeuvres looks messy, but it sounds good said out loud. We toyed with calling it 'Offline Orderves' or 'Hoff L'ine Hors D'oeuvres' but these names created as many problems as they solved. Offline Orderves made it look like we couldn't spell our own name and Hoff L'ine Hors D'oeuvres was too clever-clever; like a prog album that'd disappeared up its own arse. Besides, it didn't massively matter how the name looked written down since we'd mainly be relying on word of mouth. As long as people knew how to pronounce *hors d'oeuvres*, we were golden. Which they didn't but that's beside the point. Oh, and when I say 'we' were golden, I mean myself and Jason McKenzie.

Jason McKenzie is a first-class finger food chef. He wrote an entire letter to me about it back when we were pen pals, detailing how to match the right dip with the right snacks and how to ensure your entire buffet didn't look and taste like a bunch of better foods had shrunk and died (I believe, my classmates were reading letters about their pen pals' favourite CBBC shows or something equally trite). When I'd booked Lord Chompington's to cater my class reunion, McKenzie had got jealous and complained to me daily, 'How could you overlook me for the reunion gig? You know I'm the finger master!'

I kept telling him a) to stop calling himself that and b) that I was under the impression he only catered for his own domestic gatherings and wasn't aware he could deliver at a professional level. This was, of course, a lie. I one hundred per cent knew Jason McKenzie could deliver at a professional level but I was already making plans for Offline Hors D'oeuvres and needed to play things just right in order to get what I wanted.

Procuring a top-of-the-line finger food chef like Jason McKenzie can take some heavy negotiating, *unless* you trick them into thinking they need you more than you need them, in which case they jump on board without hesitation. I also bigged up Lord Chompington's as much as I could around McKenzie, to the point where he wanted to level the entire company to the ground. Which is exactly what we did. Jason McKenzie copied every single recipe Chompington's had brought to my reunion and EGOJAR party and improved upon them tenfold.

Over time, more and more of their clientele drifted over to us and it wasn't long before the Lord had sold the manor, as it were. On the day they finally folded, Jason McKenzie held a private party at the castle for the Tangfastic Crew to celebrate. He didn't want to cater his own party though, so hired Lord Chompington's for one final outing. They were skint so agreed and, I gotta say, the food was exquisite. It reminded me of why I'd booked them for the reunion in the first place. Lord Chompington himself (real name Craig) was bitter at first but soon got caught up in the party atmosphere and by the end had been inducted into the Tangfastic Crew along with the rest of his team. Jason McKenzie sulked for the rest of the evening. Anyway, I'm getting ahead of myself, let's go back to the early days of Offline Hors D'oeuvres and the story of how we got our very first booking.

How it's done

With McKenzie as the chef and me handling the business side of things we knew 'OO' was destined to be a success.

Sidenote: we decided to go with the double 'O' as our initials because we were scared that if we went with 'OH', people wouldn't know what the 'H' stood for (it stood for *hors d'oeuvres*, by the way). Rest assured, we brought the 'H' back into play when writing the name in full, so everybody wins.

Offline Hors D'oeuvres needed a slogan and a logo so we combined the two and came up with a slogo. It took a while but eventually we settled on a cartoon of a judge banging a gavel, accompanied by the caption, '*Hors d'oeuvres! Hors d'oeuvres!*' (a pun on 'Order! Order!', something that all judges say). We thought it was funny but everyone else told us it was shit. Apparently, just repeating one of the words featured in the name of your company 'isn't a slogo'. Mimi, a dedicated Girl Scout and the bluntest person I know, said it was like if the slogan for Mars was 'Mars! Mars!' which would've been a good point had it not immediately made me want a Mars bar, thus proving itself to be the most effective slogan ever.

Needless to say, Jason McKenzie and I refused to change the slogo because we'd already paid an artist to draw it up for us (Demetri had done it for free). We were open to changing the caption BUT it was imperative it made sense with the visual. In the end we settled on 'Do you swear to eat the food, the whole food and nothing but the food'. Pretty good, but Mimi, ever the party pooper, said it was too long and, 'The judge doesn't ask people if they swear to tell the truth, someone else does that bit, so your slogo doesn't make any sense.' Jason McKenzie and I attended a local trial, just to make sure, and Mimi was correct – the judge doesn't say that bit. This particular judge didn't even say, 'Order, order', but as he was leaving the court-room we showed him our slogo and he laughed, saying, 'Good one,' before returning to his chambers. So we kept it.

The next step was to print out our own flyers (void of con-tact details in order to remain cool) and post them through the letterboxes of everyone we've ever known, crossing our fingers they would book us for a party and, in doing so, inadver-tently invite us to their party also. We limited it to people we already knew because there's nothing worse than attending a party where you don't know anybody. We didn't fancy ending up at a stranger's eightieth, pulling teeth and clock-watching all evening. Plus if you've got a pre-existing relationship with someone, it's harder for them to tell you to get back to work.

We stuck with the drawing of the judge on the front of the flyer along with the company name. The back of the flyer was bare, save for the iconic 'OO' in the centre. This design proved to be crap. Thanks to the prominent courtroom imagery, everyone who received a flyer ignored it because they assumed it was for a French legal service. This did result in an emergency meeting where we pondered the question – should we launch our own French legal service? To begin with we were all for it, settling on the name 'Parisian Paralegals' before remembering we were currently trying to get invited to parties and the only parties lawyers got invited to were sordid affairs that would scar us for life (group intercourse and making poor people wrestle for money). So we sold our Eurostar tickets to the postman and returned our focus to the catering flyer.

We couldn't afford a completely new drawing for the flyer because we'd spent the last of our petty cash on the Parisian Paralegals T-shirts. However, we were able to give Demetri some free ribs in exchange for making some small tweaks to the existing design. In short, he turned the judge holding a gavel into a pig holding a hotdog. Before you say anything, we are fully aware of the new issues caused by this image. A pig would, most likely, not partake in a hot dog. Even if pigs do practise cannibalism, that's not exactly something you want to plant in people's minds when trying to promote your company. That being said, we did stick with the image of a cannibal pig. Above all else, we wanted to make sure the logo screamed 'food' and scream 'food' this did – it was something that would one day be food holding an item that was currently food. It couldn't be more food if it tried. If you still think it sounds stupid then get ready to shut up because two months later, we'd bagged Yvette Everson's fortieth.

Yvette Everson's Fortieth

I first met my once-Facebook friend Yvette Everson over ten years ago when we worked in the same kids' soft play centre, an establishment by the name of Pandemonium. I know I've waffled on about brand names a lot lately but I'd like to take a second to say that when it comes to company names, there is such a thing as being *too* specific. Specific to the point where you actively invite trouble. If I was starting my own soft play centre, I'd probably go with something that wasn't encouraging a lawsuit. I'd have favoured 'Safety First' or something whimsical like 'The Cautious Activity Palace' before naming the centre after a literal state of panic-inducing chaos. But what do I know, I have to ask Jason McKenzie how to spell *hors d'oeuvres* every time I write up an invoice. So maybe Pandemonium is a perfectly nice name for a place where kids are free to do as they please while their parents watch helplessly from the sidelines.

Yvette Everson was drawn to Offline Hors D'oeuvres for two reasons. 1) She's a pork fan and 2) she loves alliteration that only works when said out loud. We actually had a really good laugh about it over the phone when she made her booking (she was told our phone number by a busker she'd thrown a hunk of change to). My telephone conversation with Yvette Everson went thusly:

Yvette: All my life I've insisted my name, Yvette Everson, is alliterate and people say, 'No, Yvette – you're illiterate!'

pause

Me: So they agree with you?

Yvette: No, they . . . It works better written down, I'll text it over.

Me: I don't have a mobile phone, this is a phone box.

Yvette: OK. So, Yvette is spelt with a Y at the beginning and Everson with an E but they both sound like they start with an E when said out loud.

Me: Uh huh.

Yvette: And for this reason I say my name is alliterate as in my Christian name and my surname starts with the same letter. Alliterate with an A.

Me: Got you.

Yvette: But then my friends call me illiterate. With an I. As in, I can't read or write. Which sounds almost the same as alliterate when said out loud. So it's, like, the same problem as I have with my name and it just keeps going and going, I guess.

pause

Me: hahahahahahahahahahahahahahahahahahahahaha-hahahahahahahahahahahahahaha

To this day, I still don't get the joke. Anyway, Yvette failed to clock my voice over the phone, which was a relief as I was worried we'd lose the booking if she knew she was essentially inviting James Acaster to her birthday party. We were Facebook friends back in the day and I'd cut ties with her by chucking a full tube of Berocca in her garden pond and yelling 'orange jacuzzi'. I underestimated the power of Berocca though and what I'd anticipated to be a few bubbles turned out to be a full-blown geyser. Poor Yvette ended up with a waterlogged garden that stank of vitamin C but at least she was inside when it happened – I had to walk home drenched and smelling like a fruity fishpond. But mine and Yvette's history, it turned out, was the least of my worries.

When making the booking, I'd overlooked one massive detail: Yvette Everson and Jason McKenzie shared a birthday. One of the downsides of being off social media, and computers in general, is that you forget everybody's birthdays. You have to go back to relying on a physical calendar that you hang on the wall of the castle scullery. When I leave the house I often have to take the calendar with me, just in case somebody asks me what I'm up to over the weekend. Sometimes I have the calendar rolled up like a scroll, sticking out of my back pocket but usually I just hold it from the top, unfurled, hanging down for all to see.

Anyway, when I booked Yvette Everson's fortieth, I was still a little rusty when it came to calendar consultation. I don't mean I forgot to consult my calendar entirely, I just mean that when I did consult it, I got a little distracted. It was a *Blue Planet* calendar, you see. The photos on that calendar were so awe-inspiring that it made trivial things like birthdays seem irrelevant. How was I meant to give a shit about Isaac's 'fifteenth birthday bowling bash' when I had a photo of a blue whale swallowing a killer whale swallowing a tuna to admire? I'd dropped the ball big time. It was Jason McKenzie's sixtieth the same day as Yvette Everson's fortieth and he wanted to host an awesome party of his own. I suggested hosting Jason McKenzie's sixtieth shindig (I called it a shindig to make it sound more fun) on a different day and he flipped his goddamn lid. According to Jason McKenzie, it's 'not a birthday party if it doesn't happen on your birthday', which I said was a load of childish bullcrap but that only made matters worse. He then sarcastically asked me if I wanted to celebrate Christmas in July or go on an Easter Egg hunt next autumn. I said yes to both because I genuinely would love to do those things but he flipped his lid again and went off on a rant about building a bonfire on Pancake Day (another great idea as you'd be able to cook thousands of pancakes at once). Jason McKenzie then tried to prove to me that I knew when his birthday was by pointing it out on my calendar. Lucky for me, as soon as he laid eyes on the month of June he got entranced by the image of a tribe of calamari cleaning the tusks of a walrus by nibbling the morsels from between its gnashers and forgot why he was referring to the calendar in the first place. This proved that my actions were not malicious and he reluctantly agreed to honour the booking but remained in a huff for ages. All the days leading up to the party he was in a huff, but lightened up on the day itself because I bought him a musical birthday card that played 'Eleanor Rigby' in its entirety. The song isn't very birthday-y but Jason McKenzie likes to point at himself when Paul sings 'Father McKenzie', which he did, each and every time the song played. He opened the card sixty times in a row, one for each year he'd been alive and pointed at himself every time. I'm still astonished that I tolerated this. Each time the song drew to a close, Jason McKenzie would look satisfied then shut the card, take a beat then open it again, nodding his head to the tune and pointing to himself during the 'Father McKenzie' line. Sixty times in a row. The entire car journey from the castle to Yvette Everson's birthday party, just playing the greeting card version of that song through a tiny greeting card speaker on a loop. I managed to keep my cool but the cab driver flipped his lid pretty early on. I'd say, the fifth time the song played, he yelled at Jason McKenzie to shut the fuck up. This didn't deter McKenzie from playing 'Eleanor Rigby' another fifty-five times during the journey with the cabbie only getting angrier with each go around. In the end I managed to convince the cabbie that the best way to handle this was to stop fighting the situation and lean into it. So, for the remainder of the trip, every time Paul McCartney said 'Father McKenzie' all three of us would point at Jason McKenzie. I'm pleased to report that this seemed to calm the cabbie down, he began to accept the things he couldn't control in life and we arrived at Pandemonium safe and sound.

Pandemonium

I forgot to mention that Yvette had remained working at Pandemonium long after I'd left. She'd risen up the ranks over the years until she finally owned the place, giving her access to the soft play whenever she liked. If you ask me, soft play is wasted on the young so I fully backed Yvette's choice to host an adults-only birthday party at Pandemonium and let her mates have at it. Jason McKenzie and I arrived an hour before the guests. We walked through the main entrance, carrying the first of many platters of food, then I made eye contact with the birthday girl and we both remembered I'd once thrown a tube of Berocca in her garden pond.

Yvette flipped her lid. This was fast turning into a day full of lid flipping. A cabbie had just yelled, 'I WILL SHOVE JOHN, PAUL, GEORGE AND RINGO UP YOUR FUCKING ARSE!'

millimetres from my whimpering face and now this. Yvette was screaming bloody murder at me while Jason McKenzie set up shop next to the ball pool. I tried to calm Yvette down by playing her the soothing sounds of the Beatles but that only made matters worse. In the end we came to an agreement – Offline Hors D'oeuvres could cater the party as long as Yvette got to throw me down the highest slope in the soft play area. Yvette suggested it, I agreed in a heartbeat and within minutes she'd launched me down Mount Vertigo, a steep gradient littered with numerous padded pillars which I bounced lifelessly between like a pinball. The crash mat at the base of the mountain broke my fall despite Yvette's best efforts. She'd made sure I had some wind beneath me when releasing my limp form (she'd requested I remain limp) so it was touch and go whether I'd land inside or outside of the apparatus. I woozily clambered to my feet and gave Yvette a double thumbs up before rejoining Jason McKenzie, who was now singing 'Eleanor Rigby' out loud (who cares, it was permanently stuck in my head now anyway) and prepping a mini peppermint torte.

I'll say this – I did a very professional job organising the catering for Yvette Everson's fortieth. I was friendly, accommodating and I allowed myself to be thrown down Mount Vertigo by the birthday girl whenever she felt like it. Jason McKenzie, on the other hand, had his own definition of professionalism. Apparently, in Jason McKenzie's world, it's professional to ignore all of the client's requests and present the buffet *you* were going to have for your sixtieth instead. This meant the buffet was 100% desserts and nothing else. Don't get me wrong – this is why I like Jason McKenzie. We both love desserts and don't see the point in pretending any of the other courses are nice, especially on our special days.

Anybody, regardless of age, who eats anything savoury on their birthday quite simply does not know how to live life and it's ironic they're celebrating another year of it. For my thirty-fifth birthday (during lockdown), I'd eaten nothing but chocolate coins. The coins were from all over the world. I ate them blindfolded and correctly guessed the currency and value of each coin because I'm a chocolate connoisseur. Had this been *my* birthday party Jason McKenzie was catering for, he'd have knocked it out of the park and into the sweet shop with this puddings-only spread. But this was Yvette Everson's birthday party, a woman who had requested a Greek mezze buffet and was looking for any excuse to lob me around the soft play again. I tried to tell myself that she wouldn't notice the lack of mezze but I knew that was impossible given the state of the buffet table: seven trays of jelly, one for each colour of the rainbow, ten birthday cakes with Jason McKenzie's face printed on them in rice paper, each one full of Skittles that poured out when the cake was cut, raspberry ripple soft-serve ice cream on tap, a chocolate fountain *and* a chocolate fountain (one of them a fountain that dispensed chocolate, the other was a fountain made of chocolate that dispensed syrup). Unsurprisingly, Yvette soon flipped her lid again. Surprisingly, it wasn't at Jason McKenzie.

Yvette bizarrely *loved* the all-sweet buffet and her friends went gaga for it too. They all admitted that they only ate savoury food for show and if it was socially acceptable to eat sugary snacks non-stop, they would do it in a heartbeat. Plus the E-numbers contained within all the dishes gave them the energy required to bomb around the soft play for the rest of the day, squealing and pushing each other over while laughing like chimps. No, what Yvette Everson actually flipped her lid about was my 'mingling'. According to Yvette, she employed me to do the catering, not to attend the party myself. This presented me with a big problem. I'd started this business to get invited to more parties, not to *run a catering company*. There were guests at this party I'd not seen since I deleted my Facebook profile. Sure, most of them had no interest in talking to me since I'd welded their garage door shut or taught their dog to respond to a different name, but I was a party animal and party animals don't serve slices of Skittles cake to people – they eat the Skittles cake and do a backwards triple somersault over a gumball machine.

Yvette gave me a proper telling-off in front of everyone when I somersaulted the gumballer. I retreated to Jason McKenzie, close to tears, and told him that I now hated Yvette Everson. To demonstrate this, I threw a full tube of Berocca into the ball pool before remembering it wasn't that sort of pool. Jason McKenzie asked if this meant he had permission to fully hijack Yvette's fortieth with his own sixtieth and I said, 'Yes, do your worst.' Within minutes, Jason McKenzie had changed the '4' to a '6' on every banner, party hat and birthday card he could find, paid the DJ to play 'Eleanor Rigby' for four hours, and had the entire party singing, 'Ooooooh, Jason McKenzie' to the tune of 'Ooooooh, Jeremy Corbyn' while he swung from a series of ropes in Hysteria Jungle. He's the most charismatic man I've ever met and only he could win over the hearts of an entire party to the point where they disregard the feelings of the original host. It was epic. Yvette Everson was absolutely gutted and drowned her sorrows in jelly-bean smoothies, necking them like they were going out of fashion – which they never would because they're divine. It's Jason McKenzie's secret recipe and he refuses to tell a soul what's in them. Although, they taste like he just liquidised loads of jelly beans with a can of Irn-Bru so that's probably what it is.

Offline Hors D'oeuvres may not get another booking from Yvette Everson but one thing's for sure – I'm never forgetting Jason McKenzie's birthday as long as I live. As soon as I got home I threw my calendar in the kitchen bin. Then I retrieved it from the bin and hung it on the radiator because there were plenty more birthdays I hadn't committed to memory yet. As my calendar dried, I flipped through its pages and noticed the EGOJAR party I'd arranged over a month ago before Offline Hors D'oeuvres was even a thing. *Oh yeah!* I thought to myself, *I was meant to be spying on my ex-girlfriends!* Suddenly I couldn't think of a single reason why I would abandon such a plan so I decided to relaunch the operation while re-evaluating my approach. Trying to gather all of my exes together in one room had been way too ambitious. I needed to scale things down and, like any normal person, focus on just one ex instead. The big ex. The heartbreaker. Penelope Crouch.

Penelope Crouch

Penelope was a fun-loving, line dancing caller from Bristol and she turned my whole world upside down before flushing it down the goddamn bog. She was my most recent ex and, if I had to guess, I'd say we'd broken up two years, two months, one week, two days, eleven hours, sixteen minutes and twenty-four seconds before I came up with the idea of spying on her. The big question was: how? How do I spy on someone now I'm offline? The answer? The old-fashioned way.

The crew and I set about buying the essential bits and bobs:

binoculars, a magnifying glass, night vision goggles, fake moustache, various hats, an array of sunglasses, one walkie-talkie, climbing rope, grappling hook, zipline, head torch, dictaphone, camouflage trousers, camouflage T-shirt, black trousers, black T-shirt, some mid-market tracking devices and a few rudimentary gadgets to help me intercept phone calls and hack voicemail messages. It was tough justifying these particular purchases to Clancy Dellahue as they, in her words, 'spelt trouble'. She was very firm and said she would only give us the money if we assured her nobody would get hurt. I told her someone already did get hurt – me – and pointed to my heart. She said I made a good argument and ponied up the cash.

The most important thing when it comes to spying on your ex is to have fun with it. Personally, I utterly adored the costumes. It's imperative that you blend into the background so you're going to need a whole host of identities loaded into your bumbag and ready to go. If bumbags aren't your thing and you prefer a backpack or wheelie suitcase then be my guest but, in my experience, they'll attract unwanted attention. If you're disguised as, say, a nun or a king then a backpack will make you stick out like a sore thumb. Have you ever seen a nun wearing a backpack? It feels off. Bumbags, on the other hand, go with everything. Sure, they can be a little on the small side but I solved that by making my own custom supersized bumbag. Long story short, with just a few simple adjustments, I was able to comfortably wear a backpack round my waist. I cut off one of the straps, wore the remaining strap as a belt, allowed the bag itself to hang free and Bob's your uncle – I'd got myself a Bumpack. Patent pending on the term Bumpack but I can't see anyone competing with me on this one. The Bumpack was perfect for storing all of my disguises in – no matter what the occasion, I had an outfit for it. If Penelope was in a nightclub, then I'd don a glittery jumpsuit, star-shaped sunglasses and a perm. If she was in the library, I'd go full nerd, donning spectacles and peering at her over the top of a book (usually one of my own, allowing me to promote my work to the library clientele. *James Acaster's Classic Scrapes* and *Perfect Sound Whatever*, published by Headline, are both available in all good libraries). If Penelope was taking her car to the garage, I'd slip into a set of greasy overalls and stick a handlebar moustache onto my baby-smooth face. Then I'd intentionally break her car so I could spy on her for longer while she complained to the real mechanic. I also invested in numerous multi-coloured contact lenses because I knew Penelope could clock my dreamy eyes a mile off. I personally enjoyed going for a different colour lens in each eye as it's exactly what anyone trying to blend in *wouldn't* do. My signature contact-lens combo was one yellow cat's eye with one red cyborg eye, tied together with a strong monobrow because when it comes to disguises, it's important to establish your own distinctive style. Speaking of which – let's talk accents. Accents aren't my forte but I do a mean Bugs Bunny impression so would frequently use that voice to disguise my identity. Obviously, I tried to avoid using his famous catchphrase for fear of giving the game away but, more often than not, this proved impossible to resist. It was simply too fun to say. On the plus side, Penelope Crouch is hopeless when it comes to Bugs Bunny trivia and thinks his famous catchphrase is, 'Carrots?! What carrots?!' so the penny never dropped.

It was around this time that the Tangfastic Crew began regularly holding fancy-dress parties at the castle. This enabled me to share the wealth a little bit and let them all have a bang on my various disguises. The disguises were so good that we would often lose track of who was who and this gave the parties an added sense of jeopardy. If you lost track of which mysterious character was, for example, Sonny, then you would risk slagging him off to his face. I say Sonny because he was the only one we ever talked shit about – behind his back or otherwise. Every crew has its deadweight and Sonny was ours. Although, let me be clear – we would never kick Sonny out of the crew. Everyone is welcome in the Tangfastic Crew. Even if they're a goody-two-shoes who loves earning Scout badges and was the only member of the crew who chickened out of touching the electric eel.

Spying and why it's cool

I began spying on Penelope the week after the Yvette Everson's Fortieth and, to begin with, I liked what I saw. Even after two years, Penelope was upset and still missing me like crazy. The pandemic had clearly frozen her broken heart but now it was thawing with a vengeance and puddling in her lungs. Once, while hiding in her parents' chimney, using my feet and back to wedge myself in one fixed spot (great for your core), I heard her confiding in her mother and saying she knew she had to be strong but it was 'hard to resist phoning Jimmy every day'. I'm surprised I didn't float out of that chimney and into the sky when I heard that, that's how full of happiness and joy I was. I listened back to those words (yes, I recorded them) several times that night, while watching her sleep from the tree by her window. Small observation: exes always seem to have a tree by their window and if that's not an invitation to spy on them, I don't know what is.

It was good to feel loved again. That's what everyone forgets about being a spy – everyone loves you. James Bond is probably the most famous spy ever and people fell in love with him all the time, it comes with the territory. My favourite James Bond film is *The Spy Who Loved Me*, mainly because that's who I was to Penelope. I was the spy who loved her, just like James Bond. Except my surname is Acaster. James Acaster. Licence to spy.

After just a couple of days spying, the strangest thing happened. Penelope started enjoying her life again. Needless to say, this was torture for yours truly. I attended her line dancing class one evening (I dressed as a 57-year-old woman called Eunice, who was taking a break from her inattentive husband) and observed Penelope laughing and joking with her colleagues as well as some of the line dancing attendees. When one of my fellow middle-aged women asked me why I was weeping, I told her that my eldest, Jacob Jr, had just started university and I was worried about him. Jacob Jr had weak elbows and was quick to trust strangers, I said off the cuff. She asked what Jacob Jr was studying and I told her he was doing a master's in 'mind your own fucking business'. I was all over the place. During the next ho-down I kept mixing up my lefts and rights, turning the wrong way time and again, repeatedly ending up face to face with the ladies either side of me. They were understanding at first but soon tired of seeing the panic in my mismatched eyes and one of them told me to 'get a grip'.

I decided to cut my losses and go home after an elderly woman slid on a stray cantaloupe and stacked it pretty hard. She lay flailing on the floor, her fellow line dancers rushing to her aid as I made my way to the exit. The cantaloupe in question had just escaped my jumper where it'd been serving as a breast. I thought it best to make myself scarce before people put two and two together. I'd already aroused suspicion with my Bugs Bunny voice and something told me being one tit down wasn't about to help matters. And yes, I did tell that lady that my son was doing a master's in 'mind your own fucking business' while speaking like Bugs Bunny. And no, I can't remember if I called her 'Doc' or not. It was a rough evening. But I expect I did.

As I staggered home, comfort-eating the second cantaloupe, I took solace in the fact that, while she certainly seemed cheerier, it wasn't like Penelope had fully moved on yet. She was making friends, sure, but at least there was no boyfriend to speak of. A new boyfriend would surely destroy me.

Daniel

It was during week two that I first became aware of Daniel. He had the cleanest, shiniest shoes I'd ever seen, big powerful ankles, incredibly long legs, a weird trapezium body, a tiny little head and exceptionally clean nostrils. At least, this was how he looked from my position, belly-down on Penelope's lawn. It was night-time and I'd recently discovered that as long as I lay perfectly still on my front with a blanket of fake grass covering my body, no one ever noticed me. How invisible was I? Well, on one occasion, next door's dog dragged its itchy anus across my back (Mimi kept telling me I shouldn't be proud of this but she wasn't there). I remember peering up at Penelope and stupid Daniel as they had their first kiss. It felt like seeing Tom Space and Ernie Freedman posting on each other's walls for the first time. Scorching hot envy surged through my entire body. I wanted to get a better idea of what Daniel looked like but I couldn't tell what colour his clothes, eyes or hair were because my night vision goggles turned everything green. Quite fitting, since green is the colour of envy and I was envious as a boy can be. Can you blame me for being green with envy, though? My sweetheart had moved on, she'd found someone new, someone who made her laugh by telling amusing anecdotes about his gym buddy, Marcus. Amusing is underselling it, actually, the anecdotes were first class and I had to muffle my laughs by pushing my face into a molehill. Daniel seemed perfect and that killed me. I knew I needed to witness this guy's flaws if I was ever going to rebuild my life and get my confidence back on track. I retreated back under the sheet of fake grass, my limbs and head disappearing like a tortoise, then texted Clancy Dellahue and told her I needed more money for spy stuff.

Daniel D'Onofrio may be the happiest human being I have ever laid eyes on. Everybody loved Daniel wherever he went – the guy was kind, generous and funny as hell (see gym buddy anecdote in previous paragraph). I remember the first time I followed him to work, I couldn't believe how much his patients would brighten up as soon as he walked onto the ward. They didn't even call him doctor, they were on first name terms with the guy! 'Hello Daniel! We love you, Daniel!' they'd say. Or at least I thought that's what they said, I was usually in a full head and body cast so couldn't hear as well as I would've liked. I also couldn't move which meant whenever he wandered out of my field of vision, I was stuck looking at my bedside table, reading the 'get well soon' cards I'd cleverly written to myself – 'Wishing you a speedy recovery and hope you enjoy spying on Daniel! From, James Acaster', that sorta stuff. I soon made the decision to ditch the patient role and assume the less limiting character of a trainee nurse but this turned out to be my biggest undoing. Yes, I was able to move freely around the hospital and could hear exceptionally well thanks to my ears not being encased in plaster but I was also asked to observe several procedures as part of my training and saw things I can never unsee (I actually might be able to physically unsee them but it would involve undergoing the very procedures I was trying to forget). I thought posing as a trainee nurse would mean I got to see more of Daniel but instead it meant I got to see more of other people's poorly maintained genitalia. I'll spare you the details but, most of the time, I only knew they were genitalia because they'd been introduced as such. If I'd been shown them without any context, it would've taken me hours of guessing before landing on 'genitalia' and even then I'd be hoping I'd gotten it wrong.

Actually, while we're on the subject – many of you pervs may be wondering how you can go about looking at strangers' reproductive organs once you've quit the internet. Well, I can't recommend nursing highly enough. If celebrities accidentally sharing their own dick pics online is something you think you'll miss then my advice is to do your training, become a fully qualified nurse, move to Los Angeles and get a job in one of their finest hospitals – sooner or later, you're bound to see Chris Evans' exquisite piece (the American actor, not the English DJ. You'll probably want to pose as a Berkshire GP for a glimpse of those goods).

I wanted to learn more about Daniel's history, so I promptly smuggled myself into the clerical side of the hospital – disguised as an unassuming filing cabinet. I waited until the coast was clear and clambered out the bottom drawer to see what I could dig up on this objectively lovely man. The problem with this, and I'm still kicking myself for not foreseeing it, was that I was now out in the open without my disguise and who should walk in but everyone's favourite doctor and the funniest guy I'd ever met – Daniel. He caught me, standing in the filing room, wearing only a pair of ninja-black underwear, holding a medical assessment he'd written way back in 2012 in my clammy little paws. It was the equivalent of accidentally liking your ex's new partner's profile picture from five years ago and knowing they've seen it. My eyes then drifted to his hands and I noticed he was holding a huge stack of medical records. At first, I assumed the records needed filing but something about his manner told me this wasn't the case. The man had just caught me in my undies, trespassing in the hospital filing room and yet he was acting like it was *me* who had caught *him*.

'What have you got there, Doc?' I asked in my Bugs Bunny voice because I couldn't resist the opportunity to say 'Doc' and have it make sense, even though he clearly knew it was me so disguising my voice was pointless.

'N-nothing,' came his reply.

'Oh well, that's fair enough . . .' I began, before frisbeeing his 2012 medical assessment towards his face and lunging for the stack of records he held in his perfectly formed hands. He cried out and tried to claw them back but it was too late, I'd already seen everything and it was very damning indeed. It would appear Daniel had been doing a little light reading and decided to flick through his new girlfriend's ex-boyfriend's medical history (that's my medical history, by the way. I know that sentence is confusing).

'Oh, Daniel, Daniel, Daniel. This is a pity,' I said, insincerely because I actually thought it was brilliant. He'd looked at every X-ray I'd ever had (sixteen in total, all of my chin) and he'd basked in every illness I'd ever been on the receiving end of (including the time my eyebrows produced so much dandruff

I couldn't walk without a cane). This was quite the stalemate. We'd both caught each other with our trousers down, or, in my case, with our trousers fully off. We sized each other up, trying to figure out if we were going to have to settle this with a good old-fashioned dust-up, but as we glared into each other's eyes I noticed a smile escape Daniel's lips. The smile grew bigger, Daniel's posture softened and he began to laugh. Then I began to laugh with him. It was ludicrous! What a situation! We looked like a right couple of psychopaths and I couldn't help but see the humour in that.

Daniel and I hung out in that filing room for the rest of the day, swapping stories and bonding over how similar we were. The guy even lent me his doctor's uniform so I could easily escape the hospital (when questioned by his colleagues, he claimed his clothes had 'got some disease on them'. Daniel said he pulls that trick all the time). When I got home, I ran an idea by the Tangfastic Crew – maybe we could recruit ourselves a new member? Everyone agreed straight away. I'd been talking about Daniel all week and they'd all thought he sounded awesome. We sent Daniel a membership card and a chopping board in the post (we still couldn't shift the chopping boards from the castle gift shop so rolled them into the membership pack) and, needless to say, he accepted our invitation in a heartbeat. Mainly because Penelope found my medical records in his glovebox and had split up with him for being a weirdo. Speaking of Penelope, she has a restraining order on me now (I had planted a webcam in the same glovebox – busted!) but I don't care: I gained a new friend and that's what quitting social media is all about. Bad luck, Penelope, you may have broken my heart but I'm going to befriend every boyfriend you ever have from now on until you're single and I'm leading a gang called the EBOPC (Ex-Boyfriends of Penelope Crouch. It's not as good as EGOJAR but I was never going to get that lucky twice).

Daniel was inducted into the Tangfastic Crew on a Saturday, returned from Rhyll on a Sunday and moved into the castle on a Monday. I was with him every step of the way and I only tried to get my stuff out of storage a little bit this time.

A little warning

Little warning before we move on. When you come off of social media, not only will you have to spy on your exes the old-fashioned way but *they* will be forced to spy on *you* the old-fashioned way too. Any time I wasn't spying on Penelope, she'd be spying on yours truly, which would be fine but she was not as good a spy as I was. She didn't have any costumes, she didn't buy any of the gadgets, she would basically just hide in the bushes and watch me while wearing the same bright outfits she'd spent the rest of the day wearing. I had to pretend not to see her most of the time and concentrate on making my life look as lush as possible. The amount of energy I put into constantly making my life look lush whenever she was on the peep was mad. All I wanted to do was curl up in a ball on my bed and mourn our relationship but instead I was having to make repeated trips to the arcade, having a ball on the dance machines, playing the penny pushers with Jason McKenzie, eating a truckload of candy floss and laughing at almost everything anybody said to me (which was almost impossible since none of them were as funny as Daniel). I could always see Penelope, clear as day, peering out from behind one of those games where the mechanical claw attempts and fails to pick up a teddy bear (a metaphor for love, perhaps?), her big sad eyes letting me know she was buying my happiness act hook, line and sinker. Eventually I decided to slap a restraining order on Penelope, as it was pretty creepy having someone gawking at me all the time. I don't know if you've ever been spied on but it's very unpleasant and I hated it, hence the restraining order on Penelope the Creep AKA Creepy Crouch AKA Peeking Penny. That being said, to this day, I'll sometimes be in my living room, about to launch into a hefty sob and I'll look out the castle window and over the moat, only to see Penelope's friend Gabby crouched behind a lawn cannon, begrudgingly spying on me on Penelope's behalf. And on those nights, I put the hefty sob on hold, wake up Jason McKenzie and we head on down to Ali Baba's House of Fun to put on one heck of a show. Sometimes Daniel joins us so Gabby has double the exes to report back on. Daniel is so cool, he can push a penny like nobody's business and we have tons in common.

As soon as he came offline, Daniel began spying on Penelope every evening of the week, sharing his findings with me like a gentleman. He was loving the unplugged life but soon discovered there was something he was severely missing from social media and he wanted it back ASAP. I didn't want Daniel to regress back online so I figured out a way to help my friend stay clean and it was this action that led to my next Offline Revelation (trademark and copyright, James Acaster and Daniel).

Keeping Up with the News

The humble newspaper is dead. Shredded to death by Bill Gates, burnt to ash by Steve Jobs, then stirred into a milkshake and drunk by Sonic the Hedgehog. You can still buy yourself a humble newspaper in a humble newsagent but these days they're full of out-of-date codswallop. If you're glued to social media you get the big stories delivered to your phone as and when they happen. Then, slow as a snail riding a dead slug, the humble newspapers report the same stories the following day, by which time everyone has already made memes out of said stories and moved on to the next thing. Daniel was a real information junkie. He was missing the immediacy of global news and he couldn't simply go back to humble newspapers from humble newsagents because that would make him, in his own words, 'a Johnny-Come-Lately'. Becoming a JCL was a problem for Daniel because, also in Daniel's own words, 'No one likes that guy because he's always late to things.' The question I kept asking myself was this: how could Daniel and I receive the latest news as fast as all the brainwashed robots hooked up to their handheld devices without becoming brainwashed robots hooked up to our handheld devices? It was a question with only one conceivable answer and before I knew it, I'd purchased a police scanner.

BAWDs

Before I carry on, I can hear you all asking in your frankly irritating voices, 'But where am I meant to purchase a police scanner from?' Easy solution, you get them from a back-alley wheeler dealer. A BAWD can get you anything, any time, anywhere, no questions asked. You've probably seen these fellas in the movies. They rock up in an alleyway with a van full of dodgy stuff that nobody's legally supposed to own. You can't ask them where they got it from either as the 'no questions asked' rule goes both ways. If you treat it like a parlour game, then it's actually quite fun. The rules of the game being: try and complete the transaction without anyone asking a question. If you fail, then the other person immediately goes home and you have to either reschedule or find a new BAWD to do business with. My BAWD is a bloke named Vinny Gherkins. I first met Vinny by accident when spying on Penelope Crouch from a skip in an alleyway. I'd built myself the perfect hideout and was peeking out the top of said skip in order to watch her having a coffee with her chiropodist. Next thing I knew, Gherkins had pulled into the alley and was trying to sell me a live grenade and a crate of Colombian ghost pepper body rub. I told him I was all right at the moment but took his card anyway because it was only a matter of time before I'd be needing my own offline equivalent of the dark web. Vinny Gherkins drove a van he'd acquired from an NHS blood drive, meaning anyone who saw it just assumed he worked for the blood service. I told him about my time posing as a nurse but he wasn't impressed and called it 'irresponsible'. He had his own moral code, I guess. Vinny's card simply read: *Vinny*

Gherkins, Back Alley Wheeler Dealer, No Questions Asked.
It couldn't have been clearer. Unless, of course, your name is
Clancy Dellahue.

The police scanner was a big-money purchase so my benefactor insisted she came with. Clancy Dellahue and I met up
with Gherkins in a back alley as per. I remember Dellahue was
actually quite excited as the whole thing felt 'terribly under-
hand'. Clancy's excitement turned out to be more of a hindrance
than a help, though. She was so jazzed about buying something
naughty from such a dodgy character that she couldn't help
but ask questions. Within seconds the deal had been called off
and Vinny Gherkins had gone home due to Clancy Dellahue
asking, 'Where'd you get this police scanner from?' It took us
a grand total of seventeen attempts to buy that police scanner
because Dellahue would ask a different question every time:
'How did you become a back alley wheeler dealer?', 'Why do
they call you Vinny Gherkins?', 'Did you find that van or did
you steal it?', 'Am I seriously not allowed to ask any questions?'
But on the eighteenth attempt we managed to complete the
trade, both Gherkins and I watching Dellahue intently, our eyes
willing her not to ask anything. She nearly blew it when she
asked me where I was going to store my new police scanner but
Gherkins decided it was OK for the customers to ask each other
questions as long as he wasn't involved in the conversation. I
thanked him and as he drove away, Clancy Dellahue exclaimed,
'Bugger, I forgot to ask for a receipt.' She's quite the character.

Old Chitty

Freshly armed with our very own police scanner, Daniel and I became what I believe is referred to as ambulance chasers. The plan was simple: we slam our new gizmo on the car dashboard, listen in on the emergency services, then high-tail it to the scene of the crime – thus keeping one step ahead of the internet when it came to the next big scoop! Those of you who know my motor history may have already spotted a problem with this plan – I can't legally drive. But Daniel can. Chitty Chitty Dan Dan was a nippy lil' fella and no mistake. Daniel has asked me to point out that Chitty Chitty Dan Dan is the car's nickname and not his nickname while he is driving. His nickname while he is driving is AyrDan Senna. Jason McKenzie has also asked me to mention that *his* nickname while driving is Chasin' McCarzie. Anyway, people often write off electric cars but AyrDan really knew how to handle Old Chitty and would often let 'er rip. It was a tiny vehicle, one of those half cars that looks like it'd get decimated by the slightest dink. Every time I sat down in that passenger seat, I felt like I may as well be fired from a catapult, on a skateboard, straight onto the motorway. It felt like a giant hand had revved us up by dragging the wheels backwards along the road a few times then letting us go. But it was good for the environment and that was important to us. Plus it was incredibly easy to charge because we owned a moat full of electricity. Daniel would park Old Chitty next to the moat, chuck the cable into the flashing blue waters and watch the bars climb. If we were lucky, Enid would mistake the cable for a male eel and attempt to mate with it, fully charging the car in seconds.

Old Chitty was also the perfect spy wagon. Daniel would regularly park Old Chitty across from Penelope Crouch's house and look at her through binoculars from the comfort of the driver's seat. This could get a little boring, so he'd invite me along to keep him company. Yeah, I know – technically I wasn't allowed anywhere near Penelope but at this point the ex and I both had restraining orders on each other so, technically, she couldn't snitch me out without getting taken down herself. During those spy sessions, we would always keep the police scanner running on the dashboard. This drove the nose of Old Chitty into the road somewhat, but it was better than putting it on the parcel shelf and popping a wheelie.

We'd always have one ear on the police scanner and the other ear on the baby monitors we'd planted round Penelope's living room. Sometimes we'd confuse the two and get upset that Penelope was on the lookout for a tall man, dark hair, wearing a red hoodie and Nike trainers. Other times we'd get scared because we thought the police were specifically slagging the two of us off by name and wished we were dead.

Every so often though, we'd hear the actual cops mention something that might make for a juicy headline (loose dog in a shopping centre, overcrowding at the local swimming baths, an avalanche), so Daniel would hit the gas and we'd hotfoot it over to the crime scene. We always arrived long before social media had even got a whiff and would quickly don our reporter hats to get the full story. You will need to buy reporter hats. Trilbies or fedoras usually, with a little piece of paper stuck in the band. Once you've got your hat on, you need to pester any police, paramedics or firemen at the scene and bleed them for juicy details. Sooner or later, you'll get escorted off the premises for being 'annoying' but that's fine – they can't arrest you for being annoying. They also can't arrest you for being persistent, boneheaded or Machiavellian. They can arrest you for being cheeky though so it's best to keep track of where the line is at all times.

The best example of Daniel and I annoying the police would have to be when we turned up at our very first murder scene (!). The fuzz were already sick of us rocking up at petty burglaries and boring accidents so you can imagine how cross they were when Daniel and I strutted right into the scene of a murder, asking them if they'd found any clues yet. The victim's wife was much happier to talk to us, spilling every juicy detail until she realised we didn't work in law enforcement and rudely told us to fuck off (good luck solving anything with that attitude). The next day, everyone was talking about the murder. Clancy Dellahue informed us that it was all over social media. Daniel and I felt like gods. Long before the Twittersphere was sharing online articles about this gruesome affair, Daniel and I were talking to the widow herself and touching everything at the crime scene with our bare hands. Only the murderer, the widow and the police knew about the murder before we did (in that order). Daniel and I were officially faster than the news, faster than wireless broadband, faster than all technology. The only things we weren't faster than were police, murderers and widows – famously, the three fastest things (again, in that order).

Papermen

Obviously, as soon Daniel and I landed on a big news story we immediately wanted to share it with the world. In the old days, we would simply post a link to the article on our socials but that was no longer an option, so Daniel and I got ourselves a couple of paper rounds. We had to buy bicycles first because driving around in Old Chitty felt like cheating. We purchased two top-of-the-range mountain bikes in order to tackle the 'mountain of news' we'd be so keenly delivering. The bikes were exceptional: matching electric green affairs, each with a little orange flag on the back, flapping from a plastic flagpole. Demetri hooked us up with tons of reflectors from the road-works supply cupboard. The reflectors were a bit on the big side; the round ones were designed to top road cones and the triangles were usually placed directly onto the road to warn oncoming traffic of an accident. But the important thing was, the bikes were visible and, just like Frank Sinatra's friends when he left for New York, we could start spreading the news. We pedalled through the streets like demons, going up and down the gears as we tore round cul-de-sacs, yelling, 'Extra, extra, read all about it', and throwing rolled-up newspapers at, or around, people's homes. Most of the time they landed on the front lawn but Daniel claims he once threw one straight through someone's actual letterbox and into their house. I have no reason to doubt him.

Yeah, these were just humble newspapers we were delivering and the news wasn't as fresh as we would've liked but we were getting in some great cardio and what lazy social media bum can say that? Daniel and I were doing the equivalent of the Tour de France every single day (we called it the Tour de News) while sharing not just one article, but *all the articles* from the last twenty-four hours. Plus, and I know I've already mentioned this, we got to yell 'Extra, extra, read all about it', something that I'd always dreamt of yelling. For years, every time I shared an article on social media I would accompany it by writing, just before the link, 'Extra, extra, read all about it' but it never felt as good as hollering those words at the top of my lungs while riding James Bike-faster. James Bike-faster was my bicycle's nickname. Dan's bicycle was called Chitty Chitty Bike Bike. And when we rode our bikes we were collectively known as The Spokespeople (because bicycles have spokes and because we were delivering people the news. There's a lot of clever stuff in this book but The Spokespeople is the cleverest). Ms Mulberry, the owner of the newsagent, declared The Spokespeople to be the best paperboys she'd ever had because a) we disproportionately loved our jobs and b) we inexplicably did it for free. After a while she stopped referring to us as paperboys and, because Daniel and I were both in our thirties, started calling us what we were – papermen. Anyone can be a paperboy but hardly anyone achieves paperman status. Papermen have all the toughness of men and all the fragility of paper. Daniel and I felt like this summed us up – sensitive guys who everyone respected. The papermen. Thank you, Ms Mulberry, greatest of employers.

Celebrity Deaths

Getting ahead of the news felt tremendous but social media still beat us to the holy grail of all scoops. The white whale, the red panda, the purple hound. I refer, of course, to the celebrity death. Whenever a celeb kicks the mortal pail, social media lights up with tributes. Users compete with each other over who's the most upset, who was the biggest fan of the deceased, who can do the best oTwituary (a tweeted obituary). Such news usually gets broken on social media, announced by the celeb's family or management, so intercepting such information was certainly a big ask. Luckily for us, we're mad brainy.

We decided to work with what we had. We'd already bought phone-hacking equipment to spy on Penelope Crouch and had become quite the dab hands when it came to putting our morals to one side and hacking somebody else's phone. We also knew that celebrity agents are usually the ones who inform the public of their client's unfortunate passing, meaning someone has to tell them first. All we had to do was hack the agents' phones and wait for them to receive the devastating news from a doctor or a relative of the dead person. Or the murderer if they were killed by a show-off who likes playing cat and mouse with the feds.

I have to say, hacking a stranger's phone proved not to be as fun as hacking our ex-girlfriend's phone. Most of the agents' phone calls were about contract negotiation and a little dry for our palate. Every now and again, they would receive a panicked phone call from an insecure celeb looking for reassurance that they were 'still number one' and we'd crank up the volume. On those occasions, we'd lap up every detail: all their whacky phobias, how bad their relationships with their kids were, how much they hated Paul Merton, etc., etc. The best bit of goss we ever heard concerned one Joshua Widdicombe. Let's just say, the comedian and TV host can't stop scoffing orange Jelly Tots and he once phoned his agent in a cold sweat because he'd pilfered a packet of Tots from his infant daughter and couldn't handle the guilt. The agent got the press to drop the story by feeding them a rumour about Joel Dommett killing a man. It was the best phone call we ever hacked.

I don't want to name names but, after weeks of phone hacking, we eventually hit upon our first celebrity death and it was Tam Brillington. Tam Brillington was a part-time radio DJ who would occasionally fill in for the full-time radio DJs on Breezy FM, an easy listening station in the Greater London area. Boy, oh boy, was it easy to learn of Tam's death before anybody else. We'd heard Tam's agent, Marcy Bainbridge, speaking to Brillington's concerned wife about how Tam was in a bad way and immediately started crossing our fingers. Marcy said she'd be right there, so Daniel started up Old Chitty and we tailed her Ford Mondeo all the way to Tam's flat in East Hounslow, praying for the worst. Parking near Tam's house was a ballache, the whole area was mainly residential, but we found a side street a short walk away and arrived at his building fifteen minutes later, out of breath and hungry for a piping-hot helping of sad news. We then had to wait around the main entrance for another fifteen minutes until a resident used the front door, then we snuck in before it shut and walked the corridors until we heard sobbing echoing its way from one of the flats. Bingo was his name-o.

Here's something not a lot of people talk about. Recently bereaved people, especially if the bereavement process literally started a couple of minutes ago, hate to be asked, 'What's the latest on Tam?' especially by two strangers who've turned up on their doorstep uninvited. It was OK, though. We knew that once she saw how much Tam'd touched our lives and how much we were going to miss him, Tam's widow would appreciate we were on the same team and recognise that our grief was equal to hers. Daniel was first to express his grief to the surly widow. He talked about how he would occasionally catch Tam on the radio, usually when he expected to hear somebody else, and was so sad that it'd taken Tam's death for him to learn his name wasn't Tim. I followed this up by saying that Tam would be leaving a huge hole in my life, and that whenever I hear a DJ filling in for another DJ I will always think to myself, 'That could've been Tam if he wasn't dead.' She told us that she would miss being with him, she'd miss how the two of them could say everything to each other while saying nothing at all and she'd miss having someone in her life who truly understood her. We let her get her thoughts out of her system, then we continued to talk about the hole he would leave in *our* lives and how we, his fans and members of the public, would be forever affected by his death. Eventually, Marcy Bainbridge, super-agent, came to the door and asked us to respect the family's privacy at this time. This gave us a real kick because we were getting asked to respect the family's privacy waaay before social media was getting asked to respect the family's privacy. You could say, the only thing getting respected *more* than the family's privacy was Daniel and I. So we respectfully left the flat, drove Old Chitty round to the residents' car park and hacked the widow's phone for more details.

Remembering Tam

Daniel and I spent about two days telling everyone, as loudly as we could, how much we missed Tam Brillington. Sometimes we'd come up against a wise guy who also claimed to miss Tam Brillington and we would have to go head to head over who missed Tam Brillington the most. Don't worry, we would always win because we had visited the scene of his death and spoken to his surly widow and therefore knew way more about the situation than some 'fan' who got all their news second hand from the 'media'. The Tangfastic Crew held a memorial service for Tam and made sure his widow could see how much we missed him by holding it in the cemetery the same day as his funeral. All the candles we'd lit didn't look as impressive in broad daylight but the photos we'd chosen of Tam still held their own despite the aspect ratio being off (you could only notice the pixelation if you stood up close, though. From the funeral party's perspective, I reckon they looked legit). We made sure we matched the funeral party when it came to emotional levels. We cried when they cried and collapsed when they collapsed, we showed them that we weren't half-arsing this and cared just as much as they did. Eventually we were asked to move on. Not by Tam's family but by the family of the person whose grave we were holding the vigil on. Obviously, this struck us as odd because their dearly departed was in no way a celebrity.

From what we could make out it was just a normal guy who got old. Asking us to prioritise this nameless old dude over *The* Tam Brillington seemed pretty nuts to us, but we moved (most of) our stuff because Tam's widow sided with them and it was sort of 'her day'. Full disclosure, it took a long time to move all of the candles without extinguishing them and we had to make so many trips that we lacked the energy to also move the flowers. I know flowers don't sound heavy but there were thousands of them, all of their stems stuck through a moulded chicken-wire 3D sculpture of the word 'TAM'. It was ginormous and incredibly awkward to move, especially when you're out of breath from aggressively mourning. So we told the family we'd move the flowers another time and asked them to respect our privacy at this time.

In memoriam

Tam was the first of many celebrity deaths Daniel and I were affected by that year. It was a rough twelve months. Pottery champ Fred Wumph got off a cable car too early, furniture critic Phillipa Cheddley ingested a shuttlecock and who can forget national treasure (if the nation in question is High Wycombe) Marvin 'The Mouth' Munting, who fatally stepped on a rake. Before you start, the rake did not bounce up and hit him in the face, its teeth skewered his foot and killed him. Apparently, this is way more common and we shouldn't believe everything we see in slapstick comedy films. Show some respect.

Every time we lost a celebrity, the two of us had to go to such great lengths to show the world how hard the death had hit us. It basically became a full-time job. It didn't help that the families were often quite competitive when it came to the grieving process. It's like – Daniel and I are respecting *your* privacy so would you mind not crossing the crematorium to ask us to keep our goddamn wailing down?! We're going to miss your father's movies, including the movies we already own and can watch whenever we like, please try to understand that. But they seldom did. Anyway, I'd like to dedicate this passage of the book to all the dead celebrities. May your stars shine extra bright in celebrity heaven and I hope the ghosts of the general public are treating you with respect and adoration up there. For Tam x

Around this time, I was thinking about death *a lot* and, frankly, I needed a break from it. Spirits were low around the castle, everyone was feeling a little morbid and that was never the aim when we established the crew. Demetri was the only one who seemed to find the funerals revitalising and fun. Case in point, he actually had to leave one of the vigils because he got the giggles. His behaviour creeped most of us out, especially the younger Scouts. I asked Demetri to curb his delight at the passing of another human being, but he stuck up for himself, stating that funerals were meant to be celebrations. I wanted to tell him that they were meant to be celebrations of life and not death but knew I'd be wasting my time. The main thing I needed to focus on was pulling the crew out of the dumps and I wasn't going to do that quarrelling in a graveyard. The Tangfastic Crew needed a little trip to Opposite Town. So I decided to give the grave a rest and organise a little visit to the cradle.

How to Get Updates
on Everyone's Babies

I used to know everything about everyone's babies. There was a time when if you asked me what my specialist subject on *Mastermind* would be, I would've said, 'Everyone's babies' and then I would've won *Mastermind*. But as things currently stood, I knew nothing about anyone's babies and I was going to score zero on my specialist subject and lose *Mastermind*, embarrassing myself on national television and killing my career forever. If I was ever going to become Mastermind Grand Champion, and I'm talking proper *Mastermind* here not the stabilisers-on celebrity version, I'd need full updates on as many babies as humanly possible.

Time was, I'd get updated on my friends' babies via Facebook and Instagram, photo after video after status update charting the progress of their subjectively cute cherubs, whether I'd asked for them or not (I hadn't). But that was no longer an option since all of my new friends (the Tangfastic Crew) were baby-less: Daniel was a tragic bachelor, Jason McKenzie's kids were older than me (with the exception of his teenage son, Howard), Demetri was sterile, Lord Chompington was married to the job and the rest of the Tangfastics were virgins. This meant I had to wave goodbye to updates on my friends' babies and settle for the lowdown on any and all babies – no matter who they belonged to. I also had to do this in a way that didn't make me appear like an unsavoury character – that part was crucial. This is why I started a crèche.

Crèche time

Those of you who've actually been following my instructions should have no problem whatsoever when it comes to starting up your own crèche because you've already gone and got yourselves a crispy-fresh CRB check. If you haven't been following all the steps in this book TO THE LETTER then congratulations – you've wasted everyone's time. By 'everyone' I mean you've wasted your own time and my time. But mainly my time. I spent ages writing this book but apparently that means diddly squat to you because you're a self-obsessed little webhead who only cares about themselves. If you didn't get the CRB check when I initially told you to then I'm going to assume you ended up in prison after attempting to join the Scouts without the appropriate documentation. If you are reading this in prison, then I suggest you view whatever stretch you're currently serving as an opportunity. You're locked up, isolated from the rest of the world and the only mobile phones you can get access to have been up someone's derrière. Sounds horrendous but conditions are actually *perfect* for launching your very own Project Offline. In fact, just quickly, I'll break down *Project Offline – Prison Edition* for all the jailbirds out there:

Making New Friends

You can make plenty of new friends in the clink so find yourself a gang and do whatever it takes to be accepted by them. It won't be as fun as joining the Scouts, and the initiation ceremony will be way more disturbing, but you should've thought about that before getting yourself thrown in the Big House.

Keeping Tabs on Old Friends

I'd strongly suggest adding all of your ex-classmates to your visitation list so you can catch up with them should they choose to accept the invitation and visit you while you're inside. Most of them will say no but those who accept are most likely the weirdest of the bunch so – jackpot!

Everything Else

Spying on your ex, getting invited to parties and keeping up with the news might be trickier now you're a convict, but not impossible. Every prison has a guy who can get you anything so you should probably utilise this person as much as possible. I won't sugarcoat it, they'll have you do some pretty heinous stuff in exchange for their services but desperate times call for desperate measures so be prepared to ask your ex-classmates to lend their derrières to the cause, if you know what I mean. Smuggling a police scanner into prison is going to be quite the ask but it's doable with a little 'can do' attitude and the right walk. Once you've got said scanner in your cell, fair warning, it's going to go haywire. You're in prison, there are police everywhere, so you'll be picking up chats non-stop. But at the very least you'll be fully on top of the latest and tastiest prison news so it's fully worth the hassle.

Those of you not in prison – your CRB check currently enables you to work with kids, so if you write a nice letter to the CRB office and ask them to add babies to the deal, they'll do it free of charge.

Little Joeys

Once you've got a CRBB check (the extra B stands for Baby but I'm not sure which B it is), you'll need a solid venue for your brilliant crèche. This should be easy enough as many people start crèches out of their own home. However, I didn't person- ally want a bunch of babies munching through my brand-new castle like a plague of incontinent locusts so I convinced Jason McKenzie to let us use his place. Moving in with me had been a spur of the moment decision so McKenzie never got round to selling his old pad – a bungalow he owned outright, situated in East Sheen. Jason McKenzie was fine with me turning his place into a crèche and even gave me permission to paint flowers, butterflies and bumble bees on the window panes to make it look like the real deal. I called it 'Little Joeys' because someone (Demetri) told me it was a good idea to name a crèche after a baby animal. It shows that you have an extensive knowledge of babies – human or otherwise – so the parents know their kids are in safe hands. That's 'kids' as in human children by the way, not as in baby goats*. Since

---

* oh man, I know so much about baby animals, it's embar- rassing, I'm officially making 'baby animals' my Mastermind backup subject.

most baby animals had already been claimed by other crèches, I went for the baby kangaroo, my only other available choices being the aforementioned 'kid' or 'spiderling', both of which came with their own problems. I hoped the name Little Joeys would lead to the kids being adorably referred to as 'little joeys' but, annoyingly, everyone assumed *my* name was Little Joey instead. All the parents called me Little Joey on day one and, as I had a million other things on my mind, I failed to correct them. By day two it was too late. So they all think my name's Little Joey now. What wound me up even more was that the sign above the door didn't say 'Little Joey's Crèche', it said 'Little Joeys Crèche', with a cartoon of me smiling and giving a thumbs up underneath. The cartoon of me obviously contributed to the confusion but what really got to me was the clear lack of an apostrophe in 'Joeys'. If my name was Little Joey and this was 'Little Joey's Crèche', then the sign currently made it look like I couldn't do grammar. This irked me. The thought of the parents looking at that sign every day and thinking, *Oh dear, Little Joey really isn't the sharpest toy in the toybox*, played heavily on my mind. By day three, I'd hopped on a step ladder with a permanent marker and added an apostrophe between the 'y' and the 's' by hand. It was either that or try to draw a baby kangaroo but I did a bunch of practice joeys and without their mother they just look like lone chihuahuas so I went with the apostrophe and resigned myself to being Little Joey forever.

Little Joey's

Name confusion aside, Little Joey's Crèche was a roaring success. Within a matter of days we managed to blow our rival crèche, Ryan's Goslings, out of the water. Ryan's Goslings was run by a lady named Kiki Ryan. She was in her sixties and intentionally dressed like a literal clown – big curly hair (dyed a different unnatural colour every week) and colourful baggy clothes galore, with a wide range of quirky dungarees on heavy rotation. The day before the Little Joey's grand opening she paid me a little visit to inform me that she was going to tear my business limb from limb and leave me twitching in the gutter. I responded by informing her that I was going to cut her crèche to ribbons and let it bleed out until she had nothing left. The crèche game is pretty hardcore. I knew I had to obliterate Ryan's Goslings so I introduced an offer whereby if a parent brought their firstborn to Little Joey's then we would accept every baby they had thereafter *for free*. This was a genius offer because they still paid full price for the first baby and it'd be ages until we had to worry about the remaining part of the deal. Besides, what are the actual chances of someone getting pregnant twice? My benefactor, Clancy Dellahue, pointed out that such an offer spelt the end of our business before it'd even begun but none of us have a crystal ball so who's to say. I remember opening day and seeing all of Kiki Ryan's so-called Goslings lining up outside Jason McKenzie's bungalow, holding the hands of their deal-hungry parents, and laughing my head off. Their Gosling days were over, they were ready to become Joeys now. That's Joeys not Joey's. They weren't ready to become Joey's. Anyway. Long story short, we stole all her babies and the sweetest sight

I ever did see was Kiki Ryan tearfully scrubbing a painted caterpillar off the inside of her living room window.

Baby gossip

With Ryan's Goslings taken care of, I was able to focus on collecting as much info on other people's babies as was humanly possible, since running the crèche itself was a piece of cake. The babies usually occupied themselves by playing 'bobsled' with Jason McKenzie's roller skate collection, which freed me up to harvest baby goss from their parents at the front door. I learnt everything about those damn tots: who was crawling, who was a smiley baby, who was sleeping through the night, who had an upset tummy – Little Joey's was a baby goss goldmine or a golden baby gossmine depending on what you prefer.

I spent so long shaking the parents down for deets that I needed an extra pair of eyes to watch the actual babies for me. My brilliant pay-for-the-first-kid-get-the-rest-free deal had proved so popular that the bungalow was now chock-a-block – some rooms were solid wall-to-wall babies, all sitting on the floor shoulder-to-shoulder, row after row with vacant expressions on their faces. I made a joke to one of the parents about having a 'cramped bungalow' but since they weren't familiar with the country's premier Crowded House tribute act, my witty remark fell flat and got bugger all. Unappreciated quips aside, I badly needed someone to monitor these rugrats – just in case they did anything gossip-worthy. Fortunately for me, four members of the Tangfastic Crew were working on their babysitting badge and a bit of crèche work was sure to send their progress into the stratosphere. Once the Scouts were on board, the rest of the crew followed. I was a bit concerned about bringing Demetri in but he actually came in handy due to his inherent creepiness. The majority of us weren't great at discipline but we soon discovered we could make the babies settle down just by *showing them* Demetri. The babies would look up at his face then fall silent, paralysed by an overwhelming sense of terror, and behave themselves/tremble quietly until hometime. Some of the parents were so impressed that they requested photographs of Demetri to take home with them as a little something to threaten the kids with.

Daniel was the antithesis of Demetri. The babies would gather round, transfixed by his natural charisma, and giggle at his stories with careless abandon – even the bleak ones about how much Daniel wanted kids with Penelope Crouch before she dumped him for her sexy chiropodist. Babies mainly respond to tone, so as long as Daniel delivered the story in a bright and bouncy cadence, they'd laugh like he was Johnny Bishop live at the O2.

The Scouts, on the other hand, were a regular bunch of pranksters. One day, they thought it would be funny to tell me they had the 'greatest baby update ever', professing that one of the babies had done a double thumbs up and said 'ehhhhh' like Fonzie and I believed them because I wasn't aware we were making up what babies did these days. They strung me along about Baby Fonzie all morning, only revealing the truth when I was halfway through telling the baby's mother how amazing it was that their child could impersonate 'the late great Henry Winkler'. Oh yeah, they also told me the actor had died. At the time of writing, Henry Winkler is very much alive. Needless to say, as soon as they told me he had passed on, I made plans for his Tangfastic Vigil and emotionally told several people how much he meant to me, repeatedly claiming that Arthur Fonzerelli had made me the man I am today. Luckily, all the people I said that to were babies and won't remember.

Party pad

Now I had the Crew onboard, running a crèche turned into a walk in the park. Most of the babies favoured hanging out in Jason McKenzie's bedroom because the fluffy carpet was neon pink and they thought it was fun when the bed rose up from under the floor. Jason McKenzie was a big believer in possessions over living space. In other words, he could've comfortably afforded a semi-detached house but instead bought a bungalow and pimped it out like a mansion. Many of the babies' first words became things like 'open', 'flush', 'louder' and 'stop' thanks to the numerous voice-activated contraptions around Jason McKenzie's party pad. It was our pleasure to inform the parents that their crazy tykes had learnt to say such bangers as,

'History Channel', 'Guatemalan chocolate', 'KC and the Sunshine Band' and 'activate black light'. One of the parents did complain that his baby was 'bouncing off the walls' when he picked her up one week but was massively impressed that she'd learnt the term 'double espresso'.

All in all, Little Joey's Crèche was crushing it and we were making so much dough that I could afford to hire old Kiki Gosling as an extra pair of hands. We badly needed her as well. The Tangfastic Crew had little to no idea how to run a crèche and, while we were acing the gossip side of the venture, the actual work aspect of the gig was getting on top of us. The babies had recently learnt how to activate the underfloor heating and, since they all spent most of their time sitting on the floor, this would have the same effect on them as a heated car seat AKA the classic phantom poo. The end result would be a bungalow full of confused babies, all under the impression they need to be changed, wailing like banshees for assistance but when help arrived there was no emergency to speak of. This was happening five to ten times a day and we fell for it every time. We didn't know how to put a stop to it but Kiki Gosling solved our underfloor heating conundrum by moving the trampoline away from the underfloor heating control panel. Ms Gosling also raised a few concerns about the way we were running the place but all the things she complained about turned out to be the same things we thought were awesome so we ignored her.

Bernice

There was one baby in particular who we all became obsessed with. Her name was Bernice, she was one of those Stay Puft marshmallow babies and may have been a genius. With most of the Little Joey's tots, the goss was pretty standard: they crawled to the top of the stairs, they swallowed a marble and hadn't passed it yet, they waved at a stranger thinking it was their dad. All tremendous stuff but it gets predictable after a while and we hadn't got into the crèche game because we loved predictability. So thank God for Bernice. One week, Bernice prevented an active bank robbery. Another week she flew business class to Amsterdam by stowing away in a series of suitcases starting from her house and ending in a weed cafe on the River Amstel. Bernice was the best baby. None of the other babies could yo-yo to competition standard. None of the other babies could tell if someone was lying by studying their body language. None of the other babies had a sponsorship deal with Rolex or played the theremin. I struggled to keep up with the reasons why, but Bernice did have a sponsorship deal with Rolex. I know it sounds like hogwash but the story checks out; she was always sporting a pretty hefty Rolex on her sausagey baby wrist. Bernice was a one-in-a-million tot and I know you probably think there's going to be some sort of reveal here where it turns out Bernice was actually a fully grown adult who was passing themselves off as a baby in order to get pampered at a superb crèche, but no – she was an authentic legit baby and the most interesting legit baby any of us had ever met, including Kiki Gosling and she'd met over five thousand babies during her three decades of devoted crèche work.

I didn't fully appreciate just how impressive Bernice was until she started attending peaceful protests. The protests were something to do with wrongfully imprisoned people or GM foods (I forget which, possibly both, she multi-tasked frequently). The fact that Bernice was attending such events was admirable but it was causing tensions at home. Bernice's politics didn't exactly line up with those of her parents. Her mother thought Bernice was 'up herself' and had adopted a 'holier than thou attitude'. Bernice's mum once told us that she'd made an aeroplane sound when trying to get Bernice to eat her mashed carrots only to have Bernice refuse to eat a drop because of the damage jet planes are doing to the environment. Bernice didn't open her mouth again until her mum had offset the imaginary plane's carbon footprint by planting a single cress. After that, her mother had to impersonate a zero emissions boat every teatime. The impression was particularly good, though. We would regularly ask her to do her zero emissions boat for us and it never disappointed.

We did regretfully lose Bernice as a client in the end. She divorced her parents and moved in with a billionaire on some remote island, conducting biological research on the plant life there. This led to the publishing of her memoirs *Bernice to Meet You. To Meet You, Bernice* which inevitably topped the *New York Times* bestseller list and started a worldwide revolution. Little Joey's Crèche got a mention in the memoirs so, needless to say, we were all pretty psyched about it. We tore out the Little Joey's page and framed it. It now hangs in Jason McKenzie's kitchen, just above his deli meat slicer. It reads thusly:

'If I had one word with which to describe my crèche days, that word would be 'shambolic'. The crèche itself was located in a divorcee's bachelor pad where I was super-vised by Boy Scouts, an adult man named Little Joey, his ex-girlfriend's ex-boyfriend, the divorcee himself, a rival crèche owner whose business the others had intentionally destroyed and a terrifying ghoul. My fellow babies spent their time bobbing about on the surface of various jacuzzis and riding atop an unsupervised Roomba, while I mainly focussed on maintenance work. Everything in that bun-galow was screaming to be mended. The divorcee had left his fully stocked tool belt next to the foot spa, so I helped myself to it, wearing the belt diagonally across my body, shoulder to waist. I soon set to work fixing every faulty speaker in the bungalow, starting with those fitted into the ceiling of each room. Alas, I came to regret my own competence as, upon this job's completion, the divorcee decided to play 'Eleanor Rigby' on a never-ending loop

at maximum volume, teaching the babies to point at him during the line about Father McKenzie. Those in charge regularly invited me to join their 'crew' – an invitation I declined time and again. The five adults also allowed me to manage their tax returns. This proved quite the undertaking as Little Joey had recently launched a number of small businesses and did not own a computer. I was able to cobble together enough information about his spending by contacting an elderly woman who had, for no discernible reason, decided to fund anything Little Joey felt like doing. The rest of the grown-ups were juggling multiple jobs, all of which were managed by Little Joey. They also appeared to be living in a castle together, which they claimed as their 'office'. In all my years, completing those tax returns remains the hardest and most confusing task I've ever negotiated. As far as I'm aware, upon my departure, they simply handed this responsibility down to the next smartest baby – a child by the name of Lloyd who once chugged an entire bottle of strawberry mouthwash in one sitting.

I can only imagine how that crèche is functioning in my absence. Last I heard, Little Joey had pulled a man's pants down on live television and was being sued for it. Good for him.'

A duelling of minds

The main thing I missed when Bernice left the crèche was our debates. Bernice loved nothing more than sitting on Jason McKenzie's patio during her cigarette break and arguing the toss about any old nonsense. When Bernice bid us adieu (lit-erally – we had to look it up to know what she'd even said), she took those brilliant debates with her and that, like many of the babies we looked after, didn't sit well.

In all the decades we'd been pen pals, Jason McKenzie and I barely said a cross word to one another. So, one day, at the crèche, hungry for a debate, I told him that no bungalow should ever have seven dance mats in it'. Now obviously, I don't really think that. The fact that McKenzie devoted an entire room of his bungalow to dance mats is badass. But I needed to start a verbal dispute somehow and the dance mat thing felt like an open goal. I told him having a dance room that he occasion-ally referred to as 'The Mat Factory' was 'insane' and that all the babies thought he was pathetic. Jason McKenzie stormed out of the room, which took ages as it was one of the busier rooms in the crèche. It took him about fifteen minutes to make it to the door as he had to step over each baby while yelling, 'Outta my way, babies.' He then drove back to Tangfastic HQ in Chasin' McCarzie, locked himself in his bedroom in the east wing of the castle and refused to come out again, even for musical statues (his favourite).

It'd been a long time since I'd argued with anyone face to face. I was rusty, but I refused to believe I was beyond hope. I clearly needed to refocus and start this one again, drawing inspiration from the spats I used to have when online. That's right. It was time to dust myself off, be brave and be rude to unsuspecting strangers in public.

How Do I Argue With Strangers Now?

Let's face it – the whole reason the internet even exists is because it's not socially acceptable to go around starting arguments with total strangers in the real world. So-called 'manners' drove those of us who like to think for ourselves underground, forced to anonymously scrap it out online because calling someone a 'melt' in the queue at Sainsbury's isn't the done thing. I use this very specific example because I did it.

The Sainsbury's thing was messy. Jason McKenzie still wasn't speaking to me but Little Joey's Crèche was going from strength to strength. We'd recently secured our three hundredth customer, the bungalow was packed to the rafters, every room fit to burst with babies, and I decided to celebrate by binge-eating a bunch of items from the Sainsbury's 'Taste the Difference' range. I was under the impression that the name was a challenge so I ate every item blindfolded to see if I could taste the difference between each one, like a Coke/Pepsi kinda thing. I feel stupid saying this but the next day I strode into the supermarket and proudly informed a possibly-hungover-employee that I'd conquered the 'Taste the Difference Challenge' before handing him a framed photo of me to put on the wall of fame. He asked me to clarify what I meant by this so I got specific: I had successfully tasted the difference between the pizza and the sausages, the eggs and the cottage pie, the onion bhajis and the butter, the peas and the gateaux, and so on and so forth. The possibly-hungover-employee handed my framed photo back to me while patronisingly explaining that the name was 'more of an invitation than a challenge'. What they wanted us to taste the difference between was their products and the products of other supermarkets, not between the individual products included within the range itself.

'For example, we'd love for you to taste the difference between *our* quiche and the quiche of *another* supermarket. Not taste the difference between *our* quiche and *our* cooking chocolate.'

With that, he walked away, a smarmy grin on his face, leaving me feeling like an idiot. When I feel like an idiot I always need to self-soothe ASAP. Fortunately one of my favourite self-soothing methods happens to be shopping and I was currently standing in a massive shop – a super-shop, to be specific. I strode over to the main entrance, swiftly grabbed a shopping basket then angrily stacked it full of ice cream, intending to comfort-eat the contents in one sitting, most likely in the car park of the very Sainsbury's I was standing in. I kept on replaying the possibly-hungover-employee's patronising speech in my mind. Was this how they treated everyone who tried to taste the difference between all the items in the Taste the Difference range? I was incandescent. By the time I joined the queue I was bubbling with liquid rage. I felt like a volcano, specifically a volcano that'd just been insulted by a Sainsbury's employee, and I needed to let off some steam before I fully erupted. I'd been made to feel like a dummy and balance had to be restored to the universe, I didn't care who it was with or what it was about but I needed to destroy someone in a little back 'n' forth. In short, I needed to win an argument in order to mend my broken ego. It was at this moment that I overheard a conversation between the elderly couple in front of me, chipped in and went too hard too soon.

In my defence, it was the first time I'd had an offline argument with strangers in years and my settings were all off. I didn't know how to have a civil discussion any more and I quickly paid the price – I was asked (by the same smug possibly-but-not-necessarily-hungover-employee) to use the self-service checkouts and keep my thoughts regarding crop rotation to myself. I did as I was told but the joke was on them because I never had any thoughts regarding crop rotation to begin with! Yep, I possessed no strong feelings either way when it came to crop rotation. But it seemed to mean the world to that old guy in front of me, so I'd thrown the cat amongst the pigeons and just said the opposite of what he was saying. Then all I had to do was throw an unnecessary insult at him and wait to see if I got a reaction. Which I did. This guy was flustered; his voice went up an octave, his face changed colour, he went off on a rant about a bunch of stuff I didn't even understand because I'm not a farmer and don't fully know what crop rotation is. I was in heaven. I was in heaven, and I stayed in heaven for about five seconds before getting unfairly reprimanded by the ENTIRE QUEUE. They ganged up on me like a bunch of bullies, snitching me out to the cashier and shaming me for speaking my mind.

'Nice to know freedom of speech doesn't exist in Sainsbury's any more!' I shouted as I made my way over to the self-service checkout, aggressively scanning a multipack of fun-size Twisters.

This comment rattled everyone's cages – they thought they'd won the argument by getting me removed from the queue but now I was back on top because I was hollering about being silenced at the top of my lungs. They tried to come back at me with their 'logic' so I loudly accused them of not respecting my freedom of speech and they puked all over each other with visceral frustration. I used to adore arguing with people online but was always sad that I never got to witness their anguish first hand. Well, now, here I was, basking in a bedlam of my own making. It felt exhilarating to stand proud at the tills and watch the blood vessels throb in my enemies' temples. Regarding the thick, frothy spittle as it sprayed from their blubbering lips every time they scolded me for being 'an incomparable arsehole' or a 'dick'. I felt so alive. I'd ruined their day, I'd made a difference – I mattered. I knew I needed more of this feeling so I packed all my ice cream into a bag for life, threaded the handles along a giant Toblerone and swung it over my shoulder before stepping out into the big wide world, looking for a scrap.*

Unfortunately, my exciting new approach to spats got old, fast. I initiated a few arguments per day but they always ended the same – everyone would gang up on me and I'd be asked to leave the establishment. I've been kicked out of casinos, ice cream parlours, pet shops, funeral parlours, barbers, massage parlours, carpet warehouses, pizza parlours, orchards, tattoo parlours and more than my fair share of pubs. Little-known fact – when challenged, most people won't be able to define what a parlour is, including people who work in one and they don't respond well to being called a 'parlour poser', 'parlour

---

* That's not entirely true. First, I ate all the ice cream in the car park, sheltering in the shed where they kept the trolleys because it was raining, and then I went out into the big wide world looking for a scrap. Also, I used my Nectar card as a spoon.

prick', 'parlour pricklord' or a 'big dummy'. I also had an argument with former Arsenal midfielder Ray Parlour, but that was about fracking. Everywhere I went, everybody hated me. I was tired of all these dweebs getting on their high horses and virtue-signalling by not agreeing with me. Freedom of speech matters, man, and if we're going to save freedom of speech then I should be able to say whatever I like, whenever I feel like it, to whoever I feel like saying it to, and they should shut up, keep their opinions to themself and take it on the chin. AND YET everyone keeps restricting my freedom of speech by responding to me and disagreeing with the unresearched stuff I've said. They keep speaking for themselves and saying different stuff to what I'm saying and that is *not* how freedom of speech works. Freedom of speech means I, James Acaster, have the freedom to say all the wrong stuff in the world, all the stuff that makes no sense, all the stuff that can potentially hurt people, all the stuff that can be incredibly damaging to other people's lives, and not be challenged on it – that is true freedom: for me to be able to say objectively bad, ignorant shit with no repercussions. Everyone else is too sensitive, that's why I'll keep on saying wrong stuff until they stop hurting my feelings.

The guerrilla spats were going badly so I decided to try a different tack. I needed an environment where arguments were accepted, amongst people who wouldn't have me escorted off the premises for speaking my mind. I needed to find myself in a situation where I'd actually get *rewarded* for needlessly being a contrarian. This is why I joined my very first debate team.

The road to debating

I had to enrol at a university but it was worth it; I chose a course at random (an MA in Cultural Studies), bought a baseball cap and turned up on the first day of term looking for a debate. Debate is posh talk for argument, by the way.

Sidenote: yes, I was totally in over my head with my chosen course but that's why I chose it. I was worried that being off social media meant that I'd no longer be able to educate myself when it came to other people's experiences. Twitter, to its credit, did make it easier for me to 'listen'. All I had to do was follow the right people then read any content they posted while keeping my mouth firmly shut. It's actually never been easier to 'listen' than it is right now, probably why so many people are doing it without complaining or making out it's impossible.

Once I was offline, I didn't feel comfortable loitering around people of different genders/races/sexual orientations/classes/abilities/backgrounds/life experiences and 'listening' to them without their permission – hence the MA in Cultural Studies. What a fascinating course. I'd usually turn up late due to other commitments (curating photography exhibitions and running a catering company to name but two) but my teacher Ms Nwachukwu was an eloquent speaker who dealt with all of my questions tremendously. Every single one. I'd say I'd ask between thirty and sixty questions per lesson. My approach to questions was slightly unorthodox as I'd frame them more like statements with the subtext being that I was open to changing my mind providing she was able to convince me. My classmates didn't ask as many questions and instead took a lot of notes every time Ms Nwachukwu spoke. I, myself, didn't take any notes because I understood the best thing to do was *listen*. I didn't always remember what was said after the fact but, in the moment, I listened to every word. Except when my mind drifted or I was thinking about what to say next. There was absolutely no way I was ever going to pass the course as it was a master's and I'd never studied the subject before. But I think I more than made up for that with how much I dominated every single lesson. Plus I stuck it out way longer than some nerds who claimed to be passionate about the subject but soon refused to attend lectures for reasons unspecified. Qualification aside, I wanted to come out of the course a better person and that's the main thing – that my life gets better and I improve. At the very least, it'll enable me to talk loudly about socio-political issues in public and not worry about whether I'm wrong or not. Thank you, Ms Nwachukwu, greatest of all teachers.

The audition

The MA was going great guns but I still needed to join a debating team. Scouring the cork message board in the students' union one morning, I finally found what I was looking for. A black and white flyer featuring an image of Homer Simpson throttling Bart Simpson, Bart's eyes and tongue popping out of his head. The university debate team were looking for new members and auditions were being held the following day, in the dance studio during lunch. The mere mention of a dance studio did remind me that Jason McKenzie, my best friend in the world, had fallen out with me because I'd dissed his dance mats. It'd been a month now and he still hadn't said squat to me. It was the longest we'd gone without speaking since one of us was in primary school. But I put that out of my mind and focussed on making the team.

I attended the auditions the next day with a belly full of fire. I had spent the whole morning practising debating by disagreeing with everyone I interacted with, including my obnoxious postman who insisted I had to sign for a parcel. It might sound futile but if I could debate a postman into letting me have a parcel without signing for it, then I could debate anybody. Even if the postman didn't let me have the parcel, which he didn't, I was still a better debater for giving it a go. To be fair to me, that postman has always hated me and one day I intend to push him in the moat so Enid can zap him. He'd been mildly zapped once before, on Freedom Day when he'd pissed in the moat and some of Enid's residual electricity had travelled up his piss stream, through his urethra and caused a zapping sensation in his penis. But, if anything, getting frazzed in the nob seemed to add to his whole Freedom Day vibe so I don't count it as a proper zapping.

Moving on. The debate club audition was nerve-wracking. The dance studio felt huge and empty, primarily because I was the only person who had shown up. The debate team wasn't as popular as it used to be due to most students getting their arguing fix online. But just because I was the only person who auditioned didn't mean they'd let me in easy. The three pre-existing members sat behind a long table, the mirrored wall of the dance studio behind them, reflecting how nervous I looked as I stood before these titans, vulnerable and alone. They read my CV; I'd listed every argument I'd ever had, including my recent victory in Sainsbury's and all the parlour spats I'd been in. The leader nodded her head and looked up at me, impressed.

'It looks like you've got exactly what we need,' she said and I beamed with joy.

'I couldn't agree more,' I replied.

And, just like that, I failed my audition.

The audition, again

The next day I turned up again, this time with my game head on. I'd been focussed from the moment I woke up, not letting anyone get a single agreement out of me, including my blow-hard postman who'd tried yet again to get me to sign for my parcel and had *yet again* gone home holding the very parcel he arrived with – nice try, postie. From that day forth I vowed to never sign for a parcel ever again and made that stupid postie's life a waking nightmare.

I walked into the dance studio at lunchtime, the only candidate for the second day in a row, and placed my CV in front of them once more. It was the same CV as the previous day but I'd added that morning's argument with the postie to the list. Once again, the leader looked up at me.

'It looks like you've got exactly what we need,' she said, a little slower this time. The three of them eyed me up with great intensity until, finally, I fired back.

'No, I don't, I would be a shit addition to this team and would drag you down due to my illogically blinkered approach to everything I do.'

And, just like that, I was in. I left that dance studio feeling invincible, unreasonable and highly disagreeable, ready to shake my head at anyone who dared open their mouth to me. I was officially a Rebuttler.

The Rebuttlers

The Rebuttlers was the official name of the university's official debate team. We met every Monday for debate practice and competed against other, more weak-minded teams, on Saturdays. Monday worked best for 80 per cent of our group hence why we practised on Mondays. However, that didn't stop meetings regularly kicking off with someone suggesting we move debate club to a Wednesday. This would inevitably turn into disagreement, resulting in a debate that would last the entire duration of the meeting. Because of this, we were rather ill-equipped when it came to actual debate competitions because 'What night shall we have debate club on?' rarely came up as a subject in a competitive arena. I personally didn't care what night of the week debate club fell on as I was always tight for time regardless. Every day, in the narrow gap between the end of lectures and the start of debate club, I was having to close up the crèche then complete a full paper round, so as long as debate club wasn't on a Tuesday (Scout night), I didn't much care.

Another downside to the group constantly debating its own schedule was that said debate always devolved into more of a squabble. Which meant we ended up getting a little rusty when it came to the very basics of actual debating. One day 'Competitive Squabbling' will be a thing and The Rebuttlers will reign supreme but, as things stood, we routinely had our arses handed to us every Saturday. Still, we were all very passionate about telling people to 'fuck off' and that don't count for nothing.

Allow me to introduce you to The Rebuttlers:

Sandy Cowman – team captain, extremely organised, cruel.

Adele Villalobos – kind, weakest debater, in charge of merch.

Alexander Bung – pale, self-diagnosed sociopath, hard work.

Isaac – my friend, fourteen-year-old, literal Boy Scout.

James Acaster – AKA me, AKA The Contrary Canary.

I was given the nickname The Contrary Canary because a) I was quite contrary and b) I was always up first in the competitions. The other Rebuttlers would send me down the metaphorical coalmine to see what we were dealing with and what we were dealing with was often disqualification. You heard me right. Apparently freedom of speech doesn't even exist in a professional debate – but more on that later. Isaac was the youngest Rebuttler by some distance because he was fourteen and a literal Boy Scout. Naturally, as soon as I joined the team, I brought Isaac into the fold. I always hate being the newest member of any club, it makes me feel weak compared to the others, that's why I always bring someone else in after me so they can be the runt instead. Yes, this is also why I got Jason McKenzie to join the Scouts. I did feel bad when McKenzie got teased for saluting the Union Jack with the wrong hand but I would always thank God, and indeed the Queen, that the teasing wasn't aimed at me.

I didn't *just* recruit Isaac so he could be 'the runt', I also knew he would make a tremendous Rebuttler. I once saw Isaac argue with another Scout over whether a compass told you which way was north or which way was up and he obliterated his opponent despite being on the wrong side of the argument.

Getting Isaac, a secondary school kid, enrolled in the university was a true test of my debating skills but after calling the dean of admissions an ageist, I managed to win that war and Isaac became the youngest student in the university's history (and the youngest student in university history full stop). Isaac chose to study 'The Classics' because 'it sounded like an easy course from the title alone'. Everyone knows the classics, that's what makes them classics, so he'd most likely be familiar with the entire syllabus before attending a single lecture. Weirdly, when Isaac did attend his first lecture he received two confusing pieces of news. 1) The first classic he'd be studying was something called *Elizabeth Gaskell* by someone called Mary Barton, a novel he'd never even heard of so could hardly be a classic and 2) He was expected to bring his own copy of the novel with him which he hadn't done because he'd only just learnt this book even existed. When he raised this with his lecturer, Mr Flynn, he informed Isaac that the book had been sent to his address (The Good Castle Anti-Net) but an older gentleman had refused to sign for the package when the postman called. I advised Isaac to share someone else's copy and wait for the true classics to roll in, like *The Da Vinci Code* or *3 Feet High & Rising*.

The weakest member of The Rebuttlers, sad to say, was Adele. Adele was a lovely person and a loyal friend but was easily swayed, and being easily swayed is the worst thing you can be in a debate. We didn't have the heart to kick her off the team, though. She was good company and had made our official Rebuttlers T-shirts herself during whatever class it was she took at the uni (I want to say she was doing a PhD in T-shirts). The T-shirts looked hashtag sick: electric orange in colour with a cartoon of someone pulling a moony on the front, the team name written in a circle around the aforementioned mooner. Why a man pulling a moony? It turned out Adele was a little hazy when it came to what the word 'Rebuttlers' meant and assumed it must be butt-related. This worked out well for us though, as the cartoon summed up the attitude of the team perfectly. Naturally, Adele had to print up some extra T-shirts for our devoted fans, all of which were members of the Tangfastic Crew. Demetri, Daniel, disgraced crèche runner Kiki Gosling (now an official crew member), Lord Chompington, plus Scouts Mimi, Chris and Sonny, all turned up to every debate wearing their matching T-shirts and booing the sensitivity of our opponents. Jason McKenzie was still being a sourpuss so refused to join the Rebuttlers fan club but if he didn't want to have the best day of his life every single Saturday then that was up to him.

Merch!

The Tangfastic Crew loved The Rebuttlers so much that they invited Adele, Sandy and Alexander to join up and become official Tangfastics. The invitation was instantly RSVPed 'yes', resulting in Adele having to make a whole new batch of T-shirts, this time for the Crew itself. The Tangfastic Crew's T-shirts were gunge green in colour, 'TANGFASTIC' written across the chest in bright yellow with a number on the back to denote each individual's position in the crew. Starting with me as number one right the way down to Sonny whose T-shirt just said 'Sonny' with no number to speak of. The mooning man remained on the chest but Adele had added a laptop facing his butt, implying he was mooning the internet. I also got Adele to print some iddy-biddy Little Joey's T-shirts for the babies at the crèche. These T-shirts were brown with 'LJC' on the front and a cartoon of a kangaroo with a dummy in its mouth on the back. I'd forgotten I'd previously scrapped the whole baby kangaroo idea, so the parents were surprised by the new mascot (which they assumed was a chihuahua) and even more surprised when they realised it was mooning. But Adele couldn't be bothered to switch up the design, plus kids get their butts out all the time so the joey barely looked out of place.

Kiki Gosling still hadn't completed her official induction ceremony so we lobbed her in with The Rebuttlers. All of their devices got painted over with tar, including Sandy's Apple watch and an Alexa that got dunked right in the bucket, then we headed on down to Fill 'Em Up Rhyll 'Em Up. This visit was probably the hardest I tried to get my devices out of storage but luckily The Rebuttlers were on hand to talk me out of it. The cases they put forward for me not retrieving my devices were very compelling and reminded me why we were the best debate team in the history of telling people to 'do one'. On the way out of the FEUREU, an elderly woman yelled out of her window, 'Is that James Acaster? Didn't recognise you without a torrent of shit jokes streaming out your arse.' Normally, this would devastate me, but on this occasion I knew I had a secret weapon – The Rebuttlers. This old lady had no idea what she'd just started. I grinned up at her and waited for the rebuttling to commence. Unfortunately for me, the Rebuttler who stepped forward was Adele and the old lady wiped the floor with her. By the end of the exchange, the old lady had convinced Adele that I had lacked the experience to perform in a theatre venue all those years ago and my material had been the weakest Rhyll had ever seen. Adele also agreed that heckling was a part of stand-up comedy and if I couldn't handle it then I never should've gotten on stage in the first place. It was a long train ride back to London.

Competitions and How Unfair They Are

Now you know the players, I want to get into the debating competitions themselves. The Rebuttlers strongly prescribed to the Twitter School of Arguing, which meant we mainly got disqualified for insulting the opposition or saying something 'offensive' (usually a mixture of both! haha). We knew we couldn't carry on like this so put our heads together and came up with a brand-new approach, one that would avoid disqualification and secure our rightful places as rulers of DebateLand (fictional country). Unfortunately, the new approach only made things worse. It was a tactic I'd seen be pretty effective online and God knows why it didn't translate to the real world, but if an opponent had us on the ropes and it looked like they were poised to win the debate, we would threaten to kill them. A well-timed death threat always threw our opponents off their rhythm – suddenly they'd abandon their previous argument and shift their focus on to the threat to their own life, causing the entire debate to dissolve into a meaningless slop. The only problem with this particular debating technique was that everyone kept taking the death threats seriously. I mean, come on people! Obviously we're not going to kill anyone! We were just threatening to kill people in order to shut down their argument and win a debate and, guess what, it worked! Last time I checked this was a debating competition not a truth-telling competition. You can't even say you're going to kill someone any more without everyone going nuts. It's not like we even went into great detail or anything gruesome like that, we'd simply say, 'I'm gonna kill you,' and that'd be enough. We wouldn't even say it in an aggressive manner, we'd use a normal tone of voice and deliver 'I'm gonna kill you' as a placid statement of fact. The opponent would often become discombobulated and ask us to repeat what we just said, so we'd repeat 'I'm gonna kill you', and they'd have no comeback. *Last time I checked*, having no comeback in a debate means you lose. But nooooooo, it turns out that whenever someone has no comeback they don't do the sportsmanly thing and concede, they appeal to the officiators and get the better team chucked out of the contest for making death threats. To this day, we're the debate team with the most disqualifications to our name and we couldn't be prouder because, as far as we're concerned, every disqualification counts as a win. Adele liked that motto so much that she had it printed on the backs of our official T-shirts in block capitals so it looked like shouting (another excellent debating tactic). EVERY DISQUALIFICATION COUNTS AS A WIN. It became customary after every disqualification for The Rebuttlers to spin round, show everyone the message on our backs then, while we were there, recreate the cartoon on the front of the T-shirt. Little tip for you, if you've been disqualified, you've got nothing to lose by instantly getting your butt out because they can't disqualify you twice. Even though they can ban you from the following Saturday's competition too. Which they regularly did. Because of all the mooning.

Quarrel-Mania

The closest we ever came to a recognised win (recognised by the jobsworths and the sheeple, that is) was at Quarrel-Mania. Quarrel-Mania is the largest debating competition in the United Kingdom, it takes place in a Versatility Chamber in Clitheroe and lasts an entire fortnight. Most of the teams stayed in a lovely hotel across from the venue complete with 24-hour room service, gym, swimming pool, restaurant and bar. The Rebuttlers, accompanied by the Tangfastic Crew (minus Moody McKenzie), ended up staying with Sandy's Auntie Gina in the nearby town of Chatburn (fitting name, considering we were about to *burn* people with our confrontational *chat*). The reason we stayed in Chatburn was because our university had refused to pay for our accommodation or travel. Daniel ended up driving us in Old Chitty and it was a tight squeeze to say the least. An entire crew plus a police scanner in one of those half cars equals less space than in the Little Joey's Tropical Arts & Crafts Room. According to the university, it wasn't worth funding us as we'd only get disqualified again due to being 'the cruddiest debating team in the university's history'. The university didn't share our view when it came to disqualifications counting as wins and instead only counted wins as wins. So we all agreed to make sure Quarrel-Mania became our first 'official' victory, enabling us to win back the respect and admiration of the conformist eejits we'd be returning to.

Auntie Gina

Sandy's Auntie Gina was one of the worst people I'd ever met. Self-diagnosed sociopath Alexander Bung once walked in on Auntie Gina making an 'Ultimate Bath', something we later learnt is a bath that incorporates all soaps, shower gels, shampoos and conditioners contained within the house. This was on the day of our arrival and, since she had no toiletries of her own, she raided our suitcases, clearing out our finite supply of soaps, shower gels, shampoos and conditioners (plus a bath bomb I'd been saving in case we won). Thanks to Auntie Gina, we absolutely reeked of BO for the entire competition. This was humiliating at first as teams and punters alike gave us a wide berth in the corridors, but it ended up playing very much to our advantage.

Here's a little-known fact for you – it's really hard to argue with someone who smells distractingly bad. For the first time, our opponents were rendered speechless without us threatening to kill them. There is nothing in the rules that says you're not allowed to stink. Our fans (the Tangfastic Crew) were able to secure an entire thirty by thirty block of chairs to themselves (because they stank), meaning they could really stretch out and cheer us on without worrying about offending rival fans with their godawful breath (Auntie Gina had also partaken in an 'Ultimate Mouth Clean' using anything she could find in our wash kits that related to dental hygiene). By the end of day one we'd breezed through the first couple of rounds (a Rebuttlers personal best) and made it to the quarter-final. We headed back to Auntie Gina's to celebrate by singing 'Sweet Caroline' and watching *Coronation Street*.

Coronation Street, best show ever

While staying at Auntie Gina's rubbish house, the entire Tangfastic Crew got big into *Coronation Street*. None of us had ever bothered watching it before because we assumed we wouldn't know what was happening due to the amount of episodes we'd missed over the years. The series first began in 1960 and since I never fancied catching up on a lifetime's worth of shows in order to comprehend current plotlines and complex characters, I never watched *Coronation Street*. However, on day one, we got back to Auntie Gina's to discover her watching *Corrie* on the sofa while eating all of our food at once ('Ultimate Snack'). We decided to join her, mainly because we wanted to eat at least some of the food we'd bought, and unexpectedly got sucked into the wild world of The *Corrie* Nation. All of our fears were for nought – we instantly understood what was going on and who everyone was because what was going on was 'aggro' and who everyone was was 'aggy'.

The episode we saw began with a man and a woman walking around a rather dreary house shouting about how much they hated each other. The second scene featured two different characters, this time both men, walking round a pub shouting at each other about how much they hated each other also. The third scene teed up an argument between two women for later and the episode continued like this until everyone was in tears because their lives were awful. The Tangfastic Crew loved it. Since coming off social media, none of us had glanced at a single screen, so watching TV felt like snorting all the drugs in the world then eating a bag of candy floss and going down a water slide (Auntie Gina said this was called an 'Ultimate

Blowout'). There was some hesitation over whether we should allow ourselves to watch television but hey – it wasn't online and we weren't monks. I'd watched television throughout my childhood before the internet even existed and it was brilliant, despite what the crazy old people would tell me about it rotting my brain. Television fuelled my imagination and made the world seem big and exciting. It's the internet that rots kids' brains nowadays. Remember when The Buggles mourned the death of the wireless with 'Video Killed the Radio Star'? Well, The Internet Killed the TV Star. Who's brain's rotting now, Grandad?

Anyway, *Coronation Street* was just the kind of stuff The Rebuttlers needed to watch to get us in the zone for arguing people into a breakdown. The night before the quarter-finals we studied *Corrie* hard, going back and watching selected classic episodes that we'd missed, and made notes in preparation for the next day's battle in the arena of disagreements (Clitheroe Community Sports Hall).

Quarter-finals, baby

On the day of the quarter-finals, we turned up stinking – of confidence . . . and of not showering. We had never felt this bulletproof and were certain we were about to sail through to the semi-finals and beyond. Little did we know, the other team had cottoned on to our secret weapon and came prepared. Now, you might be expecting our rivals to turn up with pegs on their noses or facemasks to block out the smell but these guys were smarter than that. They knew it wasn't enough to block out our pong – they had to match it too – and this team stank like shit. The whole Versatility Chamber ended up smelling like the unhygienic corpse of a man who'd crapped himself to death in a bed of rotting-egg-filled skunks. Before the match even began, people were retching, puking and smashing windows (even though the windows opened easily). It was the most dramatic quarter-final in the history of Quarrel-Mania and no one had uttered a word yet. The debating topic for round one was 'The British Empire: Good or Bad?' It was a big one and with our secret weapon now null and void we had to try a different tack. Naturally, we employed all the new debating techniques we'd learnt from *Coronation Street* and let the opposition have it. We yelled at the top of our lungs, we said awful things with no regard for anyone's feelings, and at one point I quoted Peter Barlow's speech to Leanne from the Valentine's Day 2011 episode. For those of you not familiar, the speech goes thusly:

> *'Then you're deluded, so let me make this crystal clear. I despise you. I curse the day we met, and every moment we spent together after that. I don't want to see you, I don't want to hear you, I don't want to hear about you. I don't want anything to do with you. As far as I'm concerned, that bouquet in your hand may as well be a wreath.'*

It was in response to my opponent stating that the colonies' economies had crashed as a result of goods going back to Britain. With the *Corrie* quotes failing us, we were left with no choice but to return to our signature debating tactic once more. So we threatened to kill them and were disqualified.

Sidenote: it turns out there is a comeback to a death threat. On this occasion, the opposition got the Clitheroe police involved and we all had to answer questions and give fingerprints at the station before we were allowed back to Auntie Gina's house. Alexander Bung was particularly irked about this as he was pretty certain he was destined to commit a heinous crime one day and would rather the cops didn't already have his prints handy. Upon our arrival at Auntie Gina's, we discovered that she'd sold the rest of our luggage to her neighbour in order to fund another Ultimate Bath (all we saw of her was a steamed-up pair of goggles peering though a mountain of bubbles) so we climbed back in Old Chitty and drove, windows down, all the way back to London. It was our most successful competition ever.

Home sweet home

The first thing I did when we got back to Castle Anti-Net was make my way to Jason McKenzie's bedroom. The door was locked as per but I could hear him working away on his latest arts and crafts project. If I had to guess from the sound, I'd say it was a papier-mâché affair but I couldn't be certain. He still wouldn't open the door to me so I left his Tangfastic Crew T-shirt outside his room, knowing that he would find it next time he went for a wizz. I made sure to place it on the floor, face down so he could read what it said on the back: 'McKenzie – 2'. Later that night I heard his bedroom door open. There was a long pause and then I heard his soft voice from the landing say, 'Tangfastic for life,' followed by the unmistakable sound of a man putting on a T-shirt. Then I heard the sound of the bathroom door opening and then the sound of him taking a lengthy dump. We were friends again.

Rebuttlers forever

Despite a record amount of disqualifications (wins), The Rebuttlers are still raging on. I honestly can't recommend competitive arguing highly enough. Thanks to the debating club, I don't miss social media in the slightest. I still get to argue with strangers, call people cucks and threaten to kill everyone, plus I've won every single argument I've ever been in, regardless of what the PC brigade may tell you. The latest thing I got disqualified for was 'getting involved in other people's debates'. The people who run these competitions are so stuck in the past, man. They need to learn that these days, if there's a debate going on between two people, then it's a free for all and anyone's allowed to get a couple of jabs in. You don't see people on Twitter staying out of other people's arguments, do you? They roll up their sleeves, grab a wooden spoon and stir the pot. So I took it upon myself to inject a little realism into proceedings and chip in during any competitive debates that neglected to include The Rebuttlers and, guess what – I won those debates too. I'd completely derail the entire thing until everyone was arguing about something totally different then spin round and show them my butt while security escorted me out of the building. Life just keeps getting sweeter.

P.S. I have since returned to Sainsbury's to settle an old score. The entire Rubuttlers crew paid my local branch a little visit, mooned the staff and invited them to taste the difference. It was the best day of my life. Oh, and look, I know this chapter has been a little heavy on the butt imagery, along with the image of a sixty-year-old man taking a lengthy dump, but before you get all pearl-clutchy on me, may I remind you that it's no worse than the constant filth you look at online every waking hour of the day. Every other web page you visit features a photograph of a butt so get off your high horse. Butts are a part of life, on and offline. Viva la Butt. Thank you.

Television

The Tangfastic Crew loved *Coronation Street* so much that when we returned to the castle, we went back to episode one, series one (first aired 9 December 1960) and binge-watched the whole thing in a matter of days. We had to buy a television in order to do this, plus a TV licence and get the castle fitted with an aerial. The bloke who came to do all the technical stuff had clearly never seen anyone living in a castle before and wouldn't shut up about it. We get that it was novel for him but we were already tired of every Tom, Dick and Harry having their minds blown whenever they found out we lived in a brilliant castle. I might sound crotchety right now but you'd be surprised at how fast the question 'Are you a king or something?' gets old. Anyway, he whacked an aerial on top of the sturdiest turret, we gave him an official Anti-Net chopping board as a tip and sent him on his way.

Introducing a screen to the house wasn't a decision we took lightly but we voted on it and Demetri was the only 'nay'. He warned us, in a rather foreboding voice, that we were on a slippery slope.

'Be warned, for you are flirting with Beezlebub, fellow Tangfastics. Welcome one unassuming screen into your home and, before you know it, you've opened the doorway to *all* screens and *all* of the evil contained therein.'

Mimi then pointed out that Demetri owned a Tamagotchi and we all laughed at him for being a hypocrite. For the first few days, we had to protect the TV from Demetri who would frequently charge up from the basement with a bucket and a paint-roller and try tarring the screen in the name of freedom. Luckily, it was only a matter of time before he too got drawn into the dense storylines and vivid world building of the greatest TV show ever to grace this mortal realm.

Why we love *Coronation Street*

Coronation Street tore our brains inside out and turned them into scrambled eggs with the amount of revelations and plot twists stitched throughout its fine tapestry of a timeline. Why wasn't Isaac studying this in classics class?! Sustaining a TV show for multiple decades is virtually unheard of, let alone doing so while constantly generating new storylines and characters that hold a mirror up to every corner of society and prompt us to ask life's most important questions, no matter how uncomfortable they make us feel. *Elizabeth Gaskell* by Mary Barton lasted just one book, I don't even think Mary Barton managed to write a follow-up, and yet she gets awarded classic status while *Corrie* slogs it out on ITV without anyone so much as uttering the phrase 'work of unparalleled genius'. The world is unfair and everyone is stupid except me and my friends. I loved every second of *Coronation Street* and yet, the experience of watching it also made me sad, it made me feel alone, almost like I'd lost my voice. I'll explain.

Once you go offline, watching television, even with a room full of your bestest buddies, becomes the most solitary experience you've ever known. I used to regularly let the global population know what I was watching, as and when I was watching it. I'd detail how spectacular it was and reel off the emotions it awakened deep within my soul. I would tag the stars of the show in my tweets so they'd know I was enjoying their work, giving them the confidence required to keep going and film another lush episode (providing they maintain the quality). I kept a lot of TV shows afloat with my first-rate encouragement but now, in 2021, I had vanished into thin air and taken my supportive tweets with me.

I'd returned to watching TV privately, like it was some lewd and shameful activity, discussing the show with the Tangfastic Crew with but no one else. Our fandom became restricted to the castle. Without my tweets, I was worried my favourite programs would dwindle into nothingness, all because I'd selfishly stopped promoting them for free. Sure, the companies who made the shows were doing their best to publicise them, they'd likely poured a lot of cash into doing so, but a fancy-pants trailer can never compare to word of mouth. It was torture staying silent knowing that a single tweet from my old account would be worth a million billboards. I know that sounds arrogant but you have to remember that no one looks at billboards any more because everyone's staring at their phones instead so their stock has plummeted. In fact, since coming offline, I've started paying attention to billboards again and, lemme tell ya, they've evolved significantly over the years.

Billboards and how crazy they are

Since everybody stopped looking at them, billboards have gotten *messed up*. It's the wild west up there these days and anything goes. Most billboards now feature extreme nudity, many cross the line into pornography (including the ones featuring meerkats) and the slogans they're sporting are confusing, aggressive and frequently disturbing. 'Just do it or else', 'You're not worth it and you never were', 'Bird surgery literally gives you wings', 'There are some things money can't buy, for everything else there's armed robbery and a life on the lam', and who can forget 'Don't just taste the rainbow, devour it whole and consume the glucose tears of the leprechaun who birthed it'. 'Bird surgery' is exactly what it sounds like, by the way. For a small fee, a disgraced doctor will graft wings onto your back, replace your lips with a beak and cover you in feathers. They turn you into a frigging bird. It's wildly unethical, which is why they keep it off the internet and firmly on the streets.

I only mention the horror that is bird surgery to illustrate how far the billboard industry has strayed over the years. You can get away with putting even the shadiest of businesses on a billboard and no one bats an eyelid – the amount of drug dealers currently utilising billboards is astronomical. At first, I was appalled but now I'm kinda used to it. My favourite drug dealer billboard belongs to Cokey Joe. You can find it on the Hammersmith flyover: it's a picture of the man himself selling a bag of drugs to a dishevelled-looking fella in a suit, with Cokey Joe's full phone number in lieu of a slogan. Cokey Joe comes across like a nice guy to do business with and if I ever started doing drugs, he'd be my first call. He looks affable.

Also, if he doesn't deliver within twenty minutes, you get the drugs free. Can't say fairer than that.

Targeted ads

Quick thought, on the subject of advertising. Coming offline also meant I'd completely cut targeted ads out of my life, which sucked because I loved targeted ads. They made my life so easy! Based on my internet history, my purchase history and conversations my phone had illegally listened to, I used to only see adverts for products I genuinely wanted and needed. But back in the real world, no such thing existed, meaning my advertising experience quickly turned into a crapshoot. On any given day, I'd be dashing from billboard to billboard, praying something would pique my interest, but since I wasn't into meth or becoming a crow, they rarely hit the spot. The ad breaks during *Coronation Street* were a total lucky dip, too. They usually consisted of a few basic products repeating on a loop – namely, gossip magazines and lottery tickets. I mean, who did they think they were selling to?! *Corrie* fans are known devotees of complex drama and the ad guys decide to push this dross? Think it through! They should be advertising the works of Shakespeare, sophisticated tobacco pipes and those silver balls hanging from strings where the ones in the middle stay still but the balls at either end click-clack back and forth. But instead, they offer us Foxy Bingo? The mind boggles. I was going mad without my targeted ads so I decided to take matters into my own hands. Or rather – I decided to *put* matters in the hands of others. And by 'matters', I mean 'flyers'. And by 'others', I mean 'a small team of flyerers'. Newton's Cradle! I just remembered the name, it's Newton's Cradle.

That's right, I hired four flyerers to flyer me every time I left the house. I didn't want them flyering me with any old flyers though – only flyers that were of interest to me. You can do this yourself. In order to assemble the team, you will need to hold job interviews. Advertising the job can be tricky. In the end, I decided to flyer potential flyerers as they were coming out of the job centre. Now, I'm not a professional flyerer myself so I had to hire a flyerer to do this. I advertised for *this* flyerer by hiring out the billboard opposite the job centre, black text, white background, massive letters:

FLYERER WANTED. SEND CV TO CASTLE ANTI-NET, TELFORD WAY, LONDON, N16 3EL

Within a week, I'd given the job to a lady named Helga who had a rich and varied background in flyering. Her background was in receiving and not distributing but she'd received a wide variety of flyers in her lifetime and that was enough for me. I sent her to said job centre where she handed out a large stack of homemade flyers to all the job seekers that day.

The flyers simply read:

WANTED: A DEDICATED TEAM OF FLYERERS TO SOLELY FLYER ONE MAN WITH THE FLYERS OF HIS CHOICE. SEND CV TO CASTLE ANTI-NET, TELFORD WAY, LONDON, N16 3EL

After a hefty series of interviews, Stefan, Freda, Violet and George all made the cut. Over fifty people applied to be in the team and the interview process mainly consisted of the applicants hearing the full extent of the job and then turning the job down. But these four go-getters didn't give a shit how weird the job was and that's exactly what I was looking for.

I promptly lent the Flyering Squad my spy gear and told them to have at it. Those four wily bastards spied the living daylights out of me, making notes of any product names I mentioned to my friends or whatever general goods I happened to utter aloud. Every day at the crack of dawn, they would run out into the world and obtain as many flyers as possible – based on stuff they'd heard me talking about and nothing else. Finally they would get into position – each choosing a different location, all kept secret from me – then jump out at various points throughout the day and flyer me with stuff I actually wanted. The flyerers would always startle me a tad, scaring the pants off whoever I was talking to, but it was worth it to feel targeted again. Most of the flyers were about tar since I was always complaining to Demetri that we'd run out. I obviously didn't need to go spending money on tar as I already had my own hook-up and got the stuff for free. For that reason, I'd usually look at the flyer for a couple of seconds, half-read it, then throw it in the bin.

Anyway, I should get back to the matter at hand and that's talking about television. Please regard this tangent about tar-geted ads as its own ad break of sorts. Pretty clever way of structuring things when you think about it. Sometimes I even impress myself.

Television Part 2

Television was now the sole screen in my life (Etch-a-Sketch doesn't count) and, with every glance, it'd remind me of old screens past, transporting my brain back in time without me realising. I would sit watching these incredible TV shows (e.g. *Coronation Street*) then absent-mindedly go to tweet about it. The channel would change unexpectedly and I'd look down at my hand to see a remote control where my tricked brain had imagined a phone. This happened twice or thrice a show and the Tangfastic Crew would flip their lids every single time. Eventually they confiscated the remote from me and gave me a parsnip to hold instead, which solved one problem but caused another – my right hand now stank of parsnip 24/7 (literally). I couldn't walk around with a right hand stinking like a parsnip my entire life, it was impractical. I needed to find a new outlet through which I could express my TV-related joy, I had to let the world know how good television was again, my opinions needed to be heard, I had to become . . . a professional TV critic.

James Acaster: professional TV critic

First things first, I needed to buy a notepad and pen. If you're gonna be a critic, you need the proper tools. To my surprise, not a single shop had a single notepad or pen on its shelves. I quickly deduced this could only mean one thing – the internet had driven the pen and paper companies out of business. The same way that Offline Hors D'oeuvres had smashed Lord Chompington's out of the catering game. Without the necessary kit, my career as a TV critic might be over before it began. Like an unaired pilot that failed to get picked up for a full series (TV analogy).

I needed a notepad and pen badly, and I wouldn't shut up about it. This became a nightmare for my targeted flyerers. They'd listen to me saying I wanted a notepad and pen all the time, try and find flyers for notepads and pens, come up short because no one sold notepads and pens any more, then have no backup products because I didn't talk about anything else. The poor bastards had to resort to shouting, 'Buy a notepad and pen' at me at random points throughout the day. They did consider drawing up their own 'notepad and pen' flyers but drawing up a flyer would require a notepad and pen so it was back to the drawing board. Not literally, of course. Drawing boards are even rarer than notepads these days. I don't even know what they look like.

How to buy a notepad and pen in the Modern Day

If I could just find a stationery shop, everything would be OK. Time was, I'd have typed 'stationery shop' into my maps app but those days were over. I kept meaning to buy myself a real-life map but with no way of knowing where the map shops were, that was a non-starter. I was running out of ideas fast but then, just when it looked like all hope was lost, science came to the rescue.

When you come offline, all of your senses heighten. I didn't notice at first but as the weeks rolled by, I discovered I could smell a plate of meatballs from ten miles away. I could hear someone sneeze and tell you what ward it came from in the hospital across the street. I could also taste the difference between every single item in the Sainsbury's Taste the Difference range. And so it was that, one fine morning, I closed my eyes and focussed on the scent of stationery. I followed the stench of fresh, unsullied erasers, the whiff of dormant ring binders, the pong of a set of watercolours yet to meet water, until I arrived . . . at a portal to the past. I opened my eyes and found myself standing in front of an old brick wall, not a door in sight, in an alleyway next to a giant, disused shopping mall. My nose had never steered me wrong before and yet here I was, in the middle of nowhere. It was at this point that a moustached man, in suit and bowler hat, trundled up the alleyway, tipped his hat to me in greeting, and casually stepped *through* the brick wall. One moment he was saying 'good morrow', the next he'd vanished and all I could hear, with my super-strong ears, was the faint *ding-a-ling-a-ling* of a bell jangling atop a swinging door. I immediately knew what I had to do. It was time to believe. Time to have faith. I took a deep breath, reclosed my eyes, opened my nostrils and stepped forwards.

'Good day, sir, and how may I help you?' creaked a knackered old voice.

I opened my eyes to see a kindly shopkeeper stooped in front of me. He was possibly a hundred years old to the day, with a warm smile and a mucky blue work jacket that reached all the way down to his scuffed brown shoes. Row upon row of wooden shelves surrounded me, each one crammed full of quills, inkwells, every type of paper imaginable and holepunches for days. The air was dusty and the floor was the colour of old teeth. I looked up at the proprietor, he raised his eyebrows and the pencil he'd tucked behind his ear wiggled as if it had a personality all of its own.

'I'd like to buy a notepad and a pen, please . . . my good man,' I replied, taking great pleasure in referring to someone as 'my good man' for the first time and then added, 'Do you have those in stock, dear sir?'

'Do we have those in stock?' he repeated with a twinkle in his eyes. '*Do we have those in stock?*' Then he took a deep breath, 'Welllllllllllll . . .' and sang a five minute song about how they had everything in stock.

It was a charming tune with lyrics that told a story and a whimsical if slightly irritating melody. He half-skipped, half-tap-danced up and down the aisles as he sang, the pencil behind his ear swaying jauntily to the beat. Every now and then, members of his family (who also worked in the shop) would join in for a line or two, appearing from behind various display stands and ladders. The song ended with him shimmying his way behind the counter and sliding a good four feet across the freshly waxed floor, all the way to the till in one fluid motion, before producing a notepad and pen out of thin air and charging me thrupence ha'penny. What followed was a rather ugly exchange whereby I attempted to pay with modern-day money and he called me every offensive slur under the sun. I'm not going to repeat the words this old sack-of-shit squawked at me but needless to say, I'm glad that git's stuck in the past where he belongs. In the end, he agreed to swap the stationery for my shoelaces and I was thrown out of the door by his bigot of a son. I landed in a pile of refuse and lay dazed, back in the alleyway. I looked over my shoulder to see the same old plain brick wall from earlier and made sure I gave it the middle finger salute as I clambered to my feet. But I'd managed to acquire a notepad and pen and that was the main thing.

Let's get writing

Thanks to my brand-new tools, I was now able to scribe my television reviews whenever the mood struck me. That notepad and pen remain the best purchase I have ever made. I've written everything with them, including this very book. Every single copy of this book may look like it's been professionally printed but that is not the case. I insisted I handwrite every copy and my publisher agreed I could do this under the condition that it looked as good as printed. It's taken a great deal of practice and a huge amount of irreparable wrist damage but this is my handwriting now and as I pen this very sentence, I can tell you, it almost feels worth it. Want to hear something truly mysterious? This is the very same pen I bought from that horrible bastard (may he rot in Hell) all those months ago. It's never run out of ink and the notepad has never run out of paper.

Almost as if there's a little bit of magic in those pages. How curious. Hashtag winky face. Anyway, now I owned the proper kit, all I needed to do was find a publication willing to publish my TV reviews.

Sing Hosanna!

Sing Hosanna! is a self-published fanzine of sorts, produced by the more senior members of my mother's church. It contains updates on the parish, their activities, any upcoming events, as well as helpful Bible verses, brilliant prayers and various details about random charities and how to donate. I couldn't help noticing *Sing Hosanna!* was missing a TV column so I contacted the vicar, offering to review one show a week, asking only to be paid a TV show's worth of my TV licence as recompense. He did not agree to my terms but was impressed by my notepad and pen so offered me the job anyway, providing I did it pro bono. I bit his hand off. Mainly because I was relieved to secure the position without having to ask my estranged mother for a reference.

My family still weren't speaking to me since I'd burned my bridges (stealing my mother's microscooter and selling it to a thrill seeker, etc.) and I wasn't about to reconnect with them, for fear of a social media relapse. I needed to keep temptation at bay so I stayed off the main church floor and wrote all my TV columns up in the belfry. For those of you who've never been in a belfry, I'll just say this – the rumours are true. There were loads of bats up there and they were incredibly territorial. Fighting them off was futile and distracted from my work so I would just let them attack me while I wrote my reviews with my magic pen and magic notebook. Incidentally, because of all the magic, the pen and notebook never got a bat-scratch on them despite numerous attempts by the bats to claw and fang them.

The *Sing Hosanna!* team was small but dedicated. June, Olive and Mrs Norman wrote the articles and Bev was in charge of printing and stapling. They were great gals but a little on the old-fashioned side. They were of the opinion that TV reviews should be written *after* the fact, and not 'as live'. Fortunately, some of us happen to know what people want these days. I don't remember seeing people tweeting well-thought-out, reflective TV reviews back in my online days. They would tweet in-the-moment reactions to the show and reading those tweets felt like watching a TV show in itself. *Sing Hosanna!* was about to be revolutionised from the inside out and I was about to knock some old biddies' woollen socks off.

Wally Price: Limbo King

Rather than focus on the same old mega-popular shows, I wanted to give a more obscure TV programme a leg-up. This is why I dedicated my first round of TV columns to *Wally Price: Limbo King*. Don't worry if you don't know what *Wally Price: Limbo King* is, all will become clear as you read the review I've included below – my finest TV review to date. This review appeared in the 10 October 2021 edition of *Sing Hosanna!* and was the best thing in it that week (its competition was a request to pray for a sick man and a shoddily hand drawn advert, courtesy of Olive, for the parish jumble the following Sunday). My review went thusly:

WALLY PRICE: LIMBO KING – S01E05
TV REVIEW BY JAMES ACASTER

OMG I'M IN LOVE WITH THEME TUNE
CAN'T HELP SINGING ALONG

RANDOM BIRD LOL

YEAH AND YOU'D KNOW, ELIZABETH!!!!!!!!!!!

DON'T TRUST THIS SWISS GUY ANYONE ELSE
GETTING BAD VIBES???

WHERE CAN I BUY THOSE GLOW IN THE DARK JEANS
SERIOUSLY I'M IN LOVE

BABY LOOKING RIGHT AT THE CAMERA LOL

DUMB BABY

SHIIIIIIIIIIIIIIIIIIIIIIIIIIIIIIIIIIIIIIIIIIIIIIIIIIIIIIIIIIIIIIIIIIIIIIT!!!!!!!!!!!!!

WOULDN'T LAVA MELT A DOOR LIKE THAT
WHAT IS THE DOOR MADE OF

WHY DOESN'T HE JUST USE THE ENCHANTED GUN
AND TURN GHOSTS INTO ALIVE PEOPLE

TUNE!!!!!

AT LEAST IN HEAVEN I CAN SKATE!!!

PROFESSOR GERALD LOOKING TIRED AF

IS MARIO LOPEZ OK

OBVIOUS GREEN SCREEN LOL WE KNOW WHAT A TIDAL
WAVE LOOKS LIKE IRL

THAT ORGY LOOKS RUFF

IS THAT MELTED BUTTER OR FONDUE THOUGH

WHO'S THE WOMAN PLAYING THE UNICORN
IT'S BUGGING ME

I RECOGNISE HER VOICE MORE THAN HER FACE
IF THAT MAKES SENSE

PIRANHAS TO THE RESCUE!!!!!!!

WHAT WHAT WHAT WHAT WHAT WAIT WHAT

ARE THEY REALLY DOING THIS

ARE THEY REALLY DOING THIS

IS THIS THE MULTIVERSE
ARE THEY DOING THIS FOR REAL

THINGS DONT MOVE LIKE THAT IN SPACE BUT OK LOL

MOST ORGIES THIS SHOW HAS DONE IN ONE EPISODE

I CALLED IT!!!!!! TOLD YOU IT WAS TIME TRAVEL!!!!!!!!
WHAT'D I SAY

WHO'S IN THE COFFIN THOUGH

NOOOOOOO DONT LEAVE US HANGING NOOOOOOOOO

I GOTTA KNOW IS IT NEPTUNE OR ZEUS OR TAPANGA

THOSE ICE GIANTS ARE GONNA STOMP HIM
UNLESS HE CAN RECRUIT THOSE MINOTAURS
WHICH I DUNNO PROBABLY NOT

CAN'T WAIT FOR NEXT WEEK

I NEED TO KNOW THE LEPRECHAUN IS OK

PLEASE DONT BE DEAD!!!!!!!!!!!

PRAY FOR TONY PEOPLE PRAY FOR TONY

ITS AN HOUR LATER AND I CANT EVEN!!!

ANYONE ELSE WANT THE WEEK TO JUST
HURRY UP SO WE CAN FIND OUT WHO'S TALKING
TO RAMIREZ TELEPATHICALLY??

OK GOING TO BED NOW BUT LET ME KNOW
WHAT YOU THINK ABOUT THE COWBOY

IS IT ROY OR PIP OR A WILD CARD

I LOVE WALLY PRICE

I LOVE COMPETITIVE LIMBO

I LOVE THIS SHOW!!!!!!!!!!!!!!!!!!!!!!!!!!!

The series went downhill from there, they tried too hard on the fan service and the guy who played the javelin thrower looked like he was phoning it in. I reviewed one more episode then switched to reviewing *Dr Bunion's Mortuary Mishaps* instead. Unlike *Wally Price*, my column went from strength to strength. After each review was published, I'd always get eager congregation members approaching me and asking questions: 'What is this programme?', 'What made you write this?', 'Why are you here? Do you even believe in God?' The more questions the public asks, the more you've got them interested in the show, and that's how you know you've done a five-star job as a TV critic. Choirmaster Trev Barton even asked, 'How do you watch this crap?' and I gladly told him he could catch it Tuesdays at 1.12 p.m. on SPHERICAL, the UK's only live TV channel devoted to the 3D format. The 3D nature of the channel was originally unknown to me so I'm embarrassed to say my review of *Wally Price: Limbo King* episode one was my shortest and stupidest ever:

<u>WALLY PRICE: LIMBO KING – S01E01</u>
<u>TV REVIEW BY JAMES ACASTER</u>
TOO BLURRY.

Talulah Glubb

There was one member of the congregation, named Talulah Glubb, who also watched *Wally Price: Limbo King* and strongly disagreed with my greatest ever review. She gave me a right dressing-down for it and said I'd totally missed the point of the whole episode. According to Ms Glubb, the whole thing was a

metaphor for the credit crunch and the fact I didn't mention
the Joe Pesci cameo was unforgivable (and Glubb's a Christian,
remember, she doesn't just throw the term 'unforgivable' around
willy-nilly). Most insecure critics would argue their corner here
but not me – I know a potential asset when I see one. I made
Talulah Grubb the official *Sing Hosanna!* film critic (I didn't
have time to watch films as well as TV) and inducted her into
the Tangfastic Crew all at once. I also decided to show my
appreciation for the rest of my *SH!* colleagues by inducting
them into the Crew. The best part of all of this was the Crew
now had someone to make us orange squash after every activity
(thank you, Mrs Norman). Bev came up with the idea of making
our own Tangfastic Crew newsletter alongside *Sing Hosanna!*
and that really got the group jazzed. *The Tangfastic Echo* was
distributed every Friday by Daniel and I. We snuck a copy into
each rolled-up newspaper we delivered on our paper round. It
featured updates on Scout meetings, gossip from Little Joey's
Crèche and The Rebuttlers latest stats, as well as adverts for my
photography exhibitions and some wonderful correspondence
pieces written by the finest letter writer I ever did meet – Mr
Jason McKenzie. Fun fact – the old biddies became the first
members inducted into the crew who didn't have to paint over
their devices with tar. This was because they didn't own any
devices in the first place and barely had to alter their lives when
joining up. Talulah Glubb, on the other hand, absolutely hated
being in the Crew and complained about it non-stop. She was
a self-confessed technophile and became adamant that our lives
were now worse for having come offline. Every crew needs a
sceptic though. Like Doubting Thomas in the original disciples.
He kept the others on their toes and got absolutely owned
when Jesus came back from the dead and called him out. So I

let her run her mouth, knowing that one day Glubb would get equally owned by yours truly. Am I comparing myself to Jesus? Only when it comes to roasting people in order to get revenge.

The critic becomes the critiqued

The first movie Glubb reviewed for *Sing Hosanna!* just so happened to be one of my own independent films – a live Cramped Bungalow gig filmed by *moi* on *moi's* camcorder. It was screened at my local cinema for the affordable price of twenty-five English pounds (the same price as the original gig) and featured some of my best camera work yet as it's easier to get to the front when watching an overpriced tribute band in a village hall. I was all of a flutter the day the review came out. Glubb's assessment went thusly:

CRAMPED BUNGALOW LIVE @ STRUMFORD VILLAGE HALL
FILM REVIEW BY TALULAH GLUBB
PICTURE QUALITY IS AWFUL!
I'M COUNTING TEN PEOPLE IN THE AUDIENCE
OMG JUST PLAY DONT DREAM ALREADY
WHY IS THE CAMERAMAN FILMING HIMSELF SINGING?
NINE IN THE AUDIENCE NOW
THAT JOKE DOESN'T WORK IN AN EMPTY ROOM, IDIOT
ARE THEY NOT GOING TO PLAY DON'T DREAM?
DON'T TAKE THE CAMERA INTO THE BOGS WITH YOU,
    MATE, C'MON
JUST GOT THEIR NAME IS A PUN OF CROWDED HOUSE
FIRE!!!
FIRE CONTAINED. PROPS TO THE BASSIST

CAMERAMAN CHATTING TO THE BAR STAFF NOW URGH
NO ONE KNOWS WHO KIKI GOSLING IS, MATE!!!
DID THEY SERIOUSLY JUST GET AN ENCORE? THERE'S LIKE
    FOUR PEOPLE LEFT IN THE AUDIENCE
FINAL SONG, NO PRIZES FOR GUESSING WHAT IT'LL BE
I CAN'T BELIEVE THEY DIDN'T PLAY IT

As a reviewer myself, it's rare to be on the receiving end of such a vicious pasting but I had to take it on the chin. Glubb was entitled to her opinion even if it was wrong or mean. Talulah quickly became the Simon Cowell of the Tangfastic Crew – the lovable bully who tells it like it is – and we adored her for it. She absolutely shredded the crèche ('irresponsible'), our vigils ('revoltingly self-absorbed') and even The Rebuttlers ('an out-and-out embarrassment to the very concept of debate'). Most gangs would probably have kicked her out due to her copious negativity but we're not like most gangs – we're the Tangfastic Crew. Just like the internet, we believe in free speech, so if Talulah Glubb wanted to say Demetri's dungeon was a problem we were all wilfully ignoring, then she was well within her rights to do that. Obviously, there's a line. Just like Twitter, we will kick somebody out entirely if they cross that line and step over from free speech into hate speech. Which is exactly what Talulah Glubb did.

Glubb's last dance

Talulah and I were out for a stroll when one of my targeted flyerers dropped down from a tree and handed me a flyer for Ye Olde Magickal Stationery Shoppe. It made sense that they'd flyer me for it – I'd been telling everyone about this invisible shop ever since I bought my magic notepad and pen there. What didn't make sense was that Talulah Glubb took one look at the flyer, said she'd been to the very same shoppe herself, then followed it up with, 'The shopkeeper there has some refreshing political views that need reintroducing to modern society.' The next day I paid one of my flyerers to flyer Talulah with a flyer that read, 'You Are Out of The Crew'. Naturally, she kicked up a stink, claiming I was only chucking her out because she'd given my Cramped Bungalow film a scathing review. But when all's said and done, she can never prove such a thing because what goes on in my brain is only known by me. She's wrong anyway, it's because she criticised my *Wally Price: Limbo King* review in the first place. Sadly, due to her refusal to take getting kicked out of the crew graciously, all of the Tangfastics were forced to 'block' Talulah. AKA we all took out restraining orders on her and she's no longer legally allowed inside her own church. Review *THAT*, you Doubting Thomas wannabe hack.

Oversharing

All in all, becoming a TV critic for a Church of England fanzine was a real game changer for me. Sitting up in the belfry, I would sometimes hear the church service rattling away beneath me. My favourite part was whenever a member of the congregation felt compelled to stand in front of everyone else and open up about their life, asking for prayer or guidance. A lady named Amanda J. Funkly once announced that she was in a feud with a fella who did sand sculptures in the town centre. Funkly knew she was in the wrong but she found his sculptures so insufferably naff she would often kick them to pieces. The guilt had given her insomnia which in turn made her irritable and more likely to fly off the handle whenever the fella sculpted a naff sleeping dog. When pressed by the rev, Amanda J. said her main issue with the sleeping dog sculptures was that the dogs always looked wide awake so were therefore insufferably naff and begging to be kicked to pieces. I was a big fan of Amanda J. Funkly. Her fellow Chrizzos, on the other hand, clearly thought she was an awful Christian and massively judged her whenever she spoke.

Hearing a stranger spill their beans like that put me in mind of the classic Facebook overshare. I used to love it when someone I barely knew posted an extremely revealing Facebook status for all to see. This one guy named Jez, who I only ever met once (at a totally bonkers baby shower), used to regularly post about his irrational fear of banjo players. His status detailing his Uncle Hector's seventy-fifth birthday hoedown remains my favourite piece of 21st-century literature. I won't spoil it for you because I'm pretty sure they'll make it into a film one day, but there's a passage where Jez compares his life to that of the protagonist in the song 'Cotton-Eye Joe' and it is *chef's kiss*.

Sidenote: I once dated a chef and I can confirm that's exactly how they kiss. Whenever we smooched, she insisted on kissing the tips of my bunched-up fingers and nothing more, making an exaggerated 'mwah!' sound every time. We were together for ten years.

Allow me to let you in on a little secret: back in my online days, I *loved* posting the occasional overshare. Being vulnerable with people I couldn't fully trust gave me quite the thrill and God knows I love a good thrill. I once posted an emotional status about a jackdaw who was picking on me every time I left the house and seeing the 'likes' roll in from people I barely knew, let alone could confide in, felt scrumdiddlyumptious. Fast-forward to 2021 and I could feel myself hankering for an overshare or two. I could tell the Tangfastic Crew anything, which was nice but hardly what one would call 'thrilling'. If I was going to get the same kick out of airing my dirty laundry as I used to, I needed to start opening up to strangers. Otherwise it felt like I was just piling up all my dirty laundry and putting it in the washing machine, choosing the recommended cycle and cleaning everything thoroughly before hanging it up to dry on a washing line or clothes horse, and that's not a thrill – that's a household chore for chumps.

Dr Hetty Taylor

After months of telling cold callers I still had feelings for Penelope Crouch and informing taxi drivers that I sometimes kissed the mannequins in Demetri's dungeon, I finally found the perfect stranger to overshare with – my therapist.

My first session with Dr Hetty Taylor was everything I'd hoped it would be. For starters, I got to break out my Bugs Bunny impression on numerous occasions due to her being a doctor. Secondly, I overshared like a world-class champ. Even though Dr Hetty had probably 'heard it all before', I knew there was no way she wasn't loving every graphic detail that guffed out of my crazy lips. I told her about the time I stress-ate twenty-seven raw crumpets. I told her that whenever I see a nice sash I have to steal it. I even told her how I'd once tried to start a rumour that I was 'the coolest guy in town' by graffiti-ing 'James Acaster is the coolest guy in town' on the side of a bottle bank. I barely knew the woman and telling her my secrets felt like riding a roller-coaster. A rollercoaster that derails, flies hazardously through the sky, then lands on the tracks of an even scarier rollercoaster before looping-the-loop into a ravine.

As the weeks went on and my overshares got even more obscure ('I frequently swallow floss' etc.), Dr Hetty felt comfortable enough to overshare in return. This was excellent because a therapist should never open up about their own life to someone they're meant to be helping. Dr Hetty told me that she'd stopped loving her husband during their honeymoon but had always been too lazy to leave him. She revealed she'd stopped believing in God aged four when she witnessed the family goldfish devour the other family goldfish in a goldfish fight. She also told me she thought her cousin was hot. I would always respond with the kind of comments I'd seen under overshares on social media; 'Aw big hug', 'you ok hun?', and the classic sad face followed by two lowercase kisses. Needless to say, Dr Hetty soon adopted these responses when feeding back to my stories, taking our sessions all the way from inappropriate to inappropriate squared then up to inappropriate cubed and then some. The two of us were trading overshares week after week and every session felt dicey as hell. But there was a flaw in our plan that we hadn't accounted for.

The more we opened up to each other, the better we got to know one another. And the better we got to know one another, the less inappropriate it felt to open up to each other. The overshares quickly became just regular 'shares', and while that certainly felt nice, 'nice' was not the dragon we were chasing here. I'm not complaining, of course. It was lovely to make a new friend and the addition of a therapist to the Tangfastic Crew was a welcome one. Dr Hetty became the in-house agony aunt for the *Tangfastic Echo*. Being an agony aunt was not something she took lightly, as she insisted that all correspondents refer to themselves as her niece or nephew and they only ever write to her if they're in literal agony. She received letters from people post-shark attack, people currently giving birth to a child, and a man who stepped on a rake but instead of the handle flipping up and bonking him in the face, the teeth went straight through his foot. Dr Hetty also trained The Rebuttlers in a little psychological warfare which helped our debate skills no end. Whenever the other team stated their case, we would respond by saying 'it's not your fault' over and over until they broke down in tears and admitted defeat. Within a month we were World Champions.

Dr Hetty soon suggested we knock the therapy sessions on the head as a) they weren't as electrifying any more and

b) if her boss found out she'd been opening up to me, let alone joined my crew, she'd be instantly fired. We knew we needed one last blowout, the overshare to end all overshares, but it had to feel the way it used to. It had to feel perilous and we weren't going to achieve that by sharing with one another. Luckily, Dr Hetty knew just the place.

Confession

We scurried over to a Catholic church one evening and crammed ourselves into the confessional booth together.

Sidenote: originally we tried getting the vicar at my mum's church to hear our confession but he said the Church of England don't do that sort of thing.

'We basically just let everyone get away with anything and think sins aren't that big of a deal. Our motto is "each to their own",' he explained, while half-reading my latest review of the Estonian quiz show COLOSSAL BRAIN PEOPLE & THE FIGHT FOR NICE PRIZES (7.5 TV aerials out of 9).

The Catholic church turned out to be exactly what we were looking for. The priest on the other side of the grate said it was unusual to absolve two people at once but we told him we weren't looking for absolution, just a stranger with a functioning pair of ears and a judgmental heart.

'You've come to the right place, you sinful pair of scuzzbuckets,' said the Father before taking too big a bite of his Mars Duo, and into the booth we went.

To begin with, we couldn't resist saying, 'I must confess, that my loneliness is killing me now,' every time Father Douglas asked us what our confession was. We did it seventeen times in a row, we laughed every time, and Father Douglas hated it. Once we'd got Britney out of our system, Dr Hetty and I told Big Doug every screwed-up thing we'd ever thought, said or done, including the time I'd helped Dr Hetty plant drugs in a colleague's desk in order to get them fired so she could scoop up all his clients. The Father told us that we were both abhorrent sinners and if we didn't repent we would be destined for a little place called the seventh circle of Hell. This was perfect. Total vulnerability met with zero empathy. Finally, after a lifetime of thinking it was for nerds, I could see why Catholicism was so popular.

Attending confession was revelatory for me and Dr Hetty. We loved it so much that we went every single evening on the stroke of midnight and would confess our heads off for two hours minimum. I wouldn't recommend this to you however, as we attended so regularly that I soon ran out of messed-up stuff to admit to.

'Father, forgive me for I gave *Ted Lasso* a neutral review in *Sing Hosanna!*' felt a little tame compared to the goods I'd delivered in the past. I knew I had to start partaking in some proper guilt-inducing hijinks if I was going to continue getting the same buzz out of these midnight overshares. The question was – what would appal Father Douglas so much that revealing it to him would feel like skydiving into a flaming barrel of piranhas? It had to be out of order. It had to be shameful. It had to be unforgivable. Fortunately, the solution turned out to be another online activity I was yet to manifest in the real world, so it would help Project Offline. In my defence, it's probably the biggest online activity of them all. If I neglected to manifest the biggest online activity of them all then I don't think I could realistically claim that my program truly works. I'd be letting you, the reader, down if I didn't at least give it a go. So I had to do it. For your sake.

I had to become a bully.

Bullies

Look, I'm not saying I don't feel bad about this but, back when I was Jaym Baecaster, I did partake in a little something known as the unparalleled freedom of anonymous bullying. I know that sounds awful but you must remember no one actually knew who Baecaster was, which meant I could totally get away with anything, including bullying people. Therefore it was fine.

In real life I'm a wimp and being a wimp makes bullying people incredibly tricky. Even online, I could never bully someone under my own name because then they'd be able to track me down in the real world and give me my just desserts – something that's not as delicious as it sounds. The term 'just desserts' should be changed to 'just cheese boards' and I don't think I need to explain why. When I was Jaym Baecaster, I could bully to my heart's content and, thanks to the levelling power of social media, my target didn't even have to be a pipsqueak. I could pick on a bodybuilder if I felt like it. The rush I got when telling a judo master to go cry to his mama was second to none. The satisfaction of getting blocked by a bare-knuckle boxer (after calling them a 'sap') felt better than drugs. Topped only by the thrill of getting blocked by an Ultimate Fighting Champion who couldn't handle the hashtag wimpywimpyonepunch.

Being blocked used to let me know I'd made an impact on someone. I'd registered on their radar and clearly held some importance in their life. This was especially gratifying if the blocker in question was a celeb. Celebs are like golden aliens from another planet and if you can get a reaction out of them that means you're special and probably even immortal by proxy. During my Baecaster days, local radio DJ stand-in Tam Brillington had blocked me on Twitter (prior to his death). All it took was for me to tweet 'All we hear is Radio Wanker' at him. I should point out that when I was bullying Tam Brillington online I had absolutely no idea he was going to die one day. I should also point out that when Tam finally did bite the dust it was of an unrelated illness and he did not die from bullying. But still, the fact that he'd blocked me let me know I'd played a significant role in his life and this made his death all the more personal for me. Rest in peace, Tam, forever in Heaven.

Masks

Bullying online was brilliant, largely thanks to the anonymity. For this reason, I chose to do the sensible thing in the real world and bully people while wearing a mask. I'd like to say that what you're currently picturing is inaccurate and what I did was far more nuanced and skilled than you might imagine, but no – it's exactly what it sounds like.

The corner shop only stocked Avengers masks and had sold out of The Hulk so I bought a plastic Iron Man mask and hit the town on a Friday night looking for people to tease from a distance. What followed was one of the worst evenings of my life. Bullying people while wearing an Iron Man mask honestly felt like a foolproof plan to me. I thought I'd be on Easy Street but instead found myself on Difficult Road via Embarrassing Alley with a small detour down Huge Regrets Boulevard. The sight of a lone adult dressed as Iron Man weirded people out and no one could understand what I was saying as my taunts were muffled. The amount of times I got asked to repeat an insult was frankly demeaning. When I bullied them in song, they could *just about* make out the tune but never the lyrics. This meant parody songs were off the table as the target would assume I was simply singing the original. One guy, who I was referring to as a 'dire jerk', thought I was just singing Katy Perry's 'Firework' to him and it made his day. I had no choice but to resort to non-verbal bullying. This consisted of me standing there, in my Iron Man mask, doing the wanker sign at people. I kept this up for the rest of the evening until a bouncer chased me out of town.

Phase 2

As I lay breathless on top of my bed, Jason McKenzie knocked on my door to ask how the bullying went. I had to be honest with him. The mask had drawn a lot of negative attention towards me and I'd become the *victim* of bullying rather than the bully of bullying. Everyone in town had made fun of me, calling me Iron Prick and Tony Stink. Several drunks even lobbed bottles at me while yelling, 'Block *that* with your shield, mate,' which is Captain America *not* Iron Man. I was out of ideas – how does one anonymously bully people and not get called Nobert Downy Troosers in the process?

Sidenote: I only got called that once and it was when a stag do pulled my trousers down.

I knew that if anyone could save me here, it was Jason McKenzie. If I was the Iron Man of the Tangfastic Crew, Jason McKenzie was the Captain America. After much consideration, Jason McKenzie suggested that I get rid of the mask and anonymously bully people by writing cut-and-paste letters instead. That way, I could still hurt their feelings without them tracing anything back to me. This is why Jason McKenzie is a genius. Just like Tony Stark.

So just to redraft my previous analogy, I actually think Jason McKenzie is the Iron Man of Tangfastic Crew and I'm Captain America. If Captain America sometimes borrowed Iron Man's mask and did the wanker sign at people. Not sure what Avengers everyone else in the crew would be but Kiki Gosling is probably Thor because she sometimes wears a cape and doesn't trust her brother.

We agreed to post just one cut-and-paste letter at first, to see how it went down. Since The Rebuttlers had stayed at her house during Quarrel-Mania, the only address we had to hand was Sandy's Auntie Gina. Fortunately, Auntie Gina had been a dick to us, so we had no problem posting her a McKenzie/Acaster original. The letter simply read, 'You're a nerd, so absurd, and you smell like lemon curd.' We gave it a first-class stamp, sent it recorded delivery so we'd know when she received it, and then we waited. Within a week, Auntie Gina had contacted Sandy's parents and dobbed us out. Sandy's parents came down on us like a ton of bricks, threatening to pull Sandy out of The Rebuttlers and send her to one of the stricter nunneries. There was only one thing for it, we threw our magazines and scissors in the moat and, as Enid devoured them in one big gulp, we prepared to bully in plain sight.

In plain sight

Choosing who to bully was extremely difficult. Even online, I never felt comfortable bullying an actual weakling and would pick on tough guys instead (while hiding in my bedroom like a legend). Now I was out in the open, I was faced with the classic bully's dilemma – you have to bully someone weaker than you or they won't accept the bullying. When I realised this, it actually made me hate bullies a little bit. Bullies weren't as cool as they'd first appeared – they were mean, cowardly people who terrorised others just for being pathetic weeds. *Someone oughta teach them a lesson*, I thought to myself, *someone oughta bully the bullies.*

It was at this point that I remembered *Dexter*, a TV series I'd once watched and regretted because the ending was shit. The main character was a serial killer who would only kill other serial killers. He also worked for the police and would tamper with evidence to cover his tracks but it was OK because the people he was killing had all done bad things (such as killing people). I don't know how much you know about serial killers but they are essentially the ultimate bullies, so whatever worked for Dexter could work for me also. If I became a bully who only bullied other bullies then I'd be the goodest bully ever. I could have my cake and eat it too. Then steal another bully's cake and eat it right in front of them while they had a good think about why they're swiping cakes from weaker kids in the first place. However, there was one small flaw in my plan – most bullies could comfortably kick my head in. So, faced with no other option, I did what we've all fantasised over but never made a reality. I got a job at a primary school and I bullied the school bullies.

Bullying children

I lied my arse off in my interview and secured the job of school janitor. I used my real name but wore fake sideburns. This worked as a compromise between bullying as myself and bullying under an alias (also I liked the sideburns because they made me feel more like an American high school janitor, even though this was, by all accounts, an English primary school). In interviews, it's important to dazzle your prospective employer so I told the head teacher that I'd once worked as a janitor at Eton. I then let myself down by making a joke about it being 'an Eton mess' before quickly clawing things back by claiming I'd turned the school into 'an Eton tidy'. I think the 'Eton tidy' line is what secured me the job. As soon as they handed me the keys to the floor buffer, I insisted that I needed an assistant (no prizes for guessing who). I told them the school was so gross that no one could remove all the scum on their own and, in a way, I wasn't completely lying. Jason McKenzie and I were going to remove some scum, all right – we were going to remove the scum out of every corridor and every classroom in the goddamn building.

Jason McKenzie and I were one step closer to becoming the Dexters of the bully world. We worked for the school now – just like Dexter worked for the cops. But, unlike Dexter, we weren't qualified for the job in any way, shape or form. Jason McKenzie had known a few janitors during his time as a primary school teacher and said they mainly just said hello to you in the corridor, so we leant into that and this kept people off our back.

During the first week we didn't bully anyone, instead we

observed the kids to see who the bullies were and, lemme tell
ya, we were spoilt for choice. As soon as the teachers' backs
were turned, those mean, sack-a-shit kids did things to each
other that brought a tear to my eye. Dead arms, dead legs,
dead necks, we saw it all. We wanted to step in straight away
but we knew we had to bide our time, plus the janitorial work
was rapidly getting on top of us. These kids littered constantly.
In my opinion, we've been blaming the wrong generation for
global warming, that's how much litter they dropped. In the
end, we decided to let the school self-clean as it seemed like
the most natural option. Also, Headmaster Brown had zero
backbone and never once raised the appalling state of the
building with us. This meant we got to focus on our true
passion – bullying – and soon narrowed down which child we
were going to bully. After much consideration, we settled on
Ivan Martin – an eight-year-old and a prick.

Ivan Martin

Ivan Martin despised wimps. McKenzie and I observed him
every playtime, cornering little Callum Michaels by the toy
shed and making him flinch with fake punches while calling
him 'Cal-bum My-balls'. The nickname made no sense but the
kid was eight and was clearly trying his best. Anyway, one day
we threw a fully inflated basketball at his head.

The school bell had already sounded, poor Callum had
retreated back to class in tears, all the other kids had run
inside, and, as usual, Ivan was sauntering behind, taking his
time because he knew the teachers didn't bother telling him off
for being late any more. The basketball didn't do any damage

but it stopped him in his tracks. McKenzie had launched it from some distance, a two-handed overhead throw, and it doinked off the kid's temple in a highly satisfying manner.

Ivan turned and looked at us, a custodial duo with matching overalls and matching fake sideburns, and asked what the fuck that was for. And then we basically bullied him for a good five minutes. It was pretty standard stuff, we called him Ivan Fartin, Farting Martin, Ivan To-eat-a-bag-a-shit – the classics – and then walked around doing derogatory impressions of him where we put on an obnoxious voice and exaggerated his clumsy-ass walk. For a bully, he cried pretty easily. Mission accomplished.

The Pay-off

That night, on the stroke of midnight, Jason McKenzie and I crammed into Father Douglas's confessional booth to do a little oversharing. We told him all about how we'd bullied Ivan Martin, how we'd lied in our job interviews and how we were putting no effort whatsoever into cleaning a school. Father Douglas went through the roof (probably why church roofs need fixing all the time lol). He said this was the lowest I or any of my 'demented little friends' had ever sunk. It was the best overshare of my life but Father D did make me feel a tad guilty. He made a good point about the kid only being eight years old and the two of us being thirty-six and 'eighty or however old that one is'. Anything poor Ivan did was likely a result of awful parenting, making him undeserving of being harassed by a couple of fake janitors chasing the high they used to get from online bullying. Bottom line, we'd mentally scarred a kid for life and, while that had resulted in an over-

share for the ages, we should probably make amends ASAP.
Papa Dougie then yelled at me again. This time for referring to
him by a bunch of irritating nicknames during our most recent
sessions, stating that his name was Father Douglas and not
Father D, Papa Dougie, Big Daddy Doug-Doug, Sweet Poppy
Doogle or Prayers McHoly. We tried to smooth things over
with the right honourable Reverend Angry by offering him a
complimentary pair of fake sideburns and, although resistant
at first, he did eventually let us post them through the grate,
providing we leave immediately. Men of our word, we did just
that, stealing a figurine of the Virgin Mary on our way out so
we had something to confess next time.

Extending the olive branch

At playtime the following day, we observed Ivan Martin sitting
alone on a wall, leaving Callum Michaels alone completely.
Callum certainly looked happier now. He was wearing a velvet
top hat, which he wouldn't have dared do before, and singing
'The Only Way is Up' by Yazz. All well and good, but there
was a chance we'd ruined young Ivan's life forever. We were in
a royal pickle. A catch-22 but worse. Maybe a catch-23 or even
a catch-24. We wanted to keep on bullying, sure, but hadn't
anticipated how much bullying a little kid would weigh on the
old conscience. Luckily, Jason McKenzie suggested a plan so
perfect it made me think we should've applied for the job of
head teacher instead of whatever it was we were meant to be
doing. First, we approached Ivan, causing him to panic and
topple backwards, falling off the wall and into some brambles.
McKenzie and I had been told several times to clip the bramble

bush but never got round to it. This is why, regrettably, the brambles were extra stabby that day. We hauled Ivan to his feet, apologised for yesterday's top-shelf bullying, then pitched him Jason McKenzie's new idea. A solution to both our problems. Ivan wanted to bully people, we wanted to bully bullies. Ivan didn't want to be bullied by adults, we no longer wanted to bully little kids. Ivan couldn't bully little kids because we would bully him for it. We couldn't bully adults because they would punch us in the face. But, you know who an adult probably wouldn't punch? A child they've only just met.

The plan was simple, Jason McKenzie and I would select a grown-up bully who deserved a good bullying, we'd give Ivan a bunch of ammunition, then send him in to bully them while we watched from a safe hiding place (e.g. a non-brambly bush). This way, all three of us got to bully people, Jason McKenzie and I got to remain anonymous, the target always deserved it and, most likely, no one would punch a kid. Later that day at home time, we inducted Ivan into the Tangfastic Crew and gave him his T-shirt. We conducted the ceremony in the school's Versatility Chamber and got him to swear his allegiance to the crew on a Bible we stole from Pappy Dougalicious's church. Ivan didn't own a phone or a laptop so we painted over his school books with tar instead. The Tangfastic Crew had finally found its Hulk and he was ready to smash. We told Ivan to meet us at the pub that evening for our first round of bullying. He then informed us that he was unable to come and meet us at a pub on his own, especially on a school night, because he was an eight-year-old child. He then cracked up and said, 'Only joking, of course I can, my parents don't give a shit about me!' Ivan was all right.

Keith Morris

Our first target was Keith Morris – my old secondary school bully and modern-day conspiracy theorist. I had recently learnt everything there was to know about Keith thanks to the school reunion I'd organised, as well as the flyers he'd subsequently Blu-tacked to my drawbridge. The flyers warned me of the government's plan to microchip my stomach and monitor my diet until I'm only eating 'European scran'. When I was twelve, Keith stole and ate an entire sandwich out of my lunchbox without even removing the clingfilm. If memory serves, he chewed it for an hour before opting to swallow it whole. He deserved everything we were about to throw at him. I knew where Keith worked, where he lived, where he liked to drink of an evening and who he believed was poisoning his tap water (the government, working together with the water, tap and poison companies). It was go time.

We unleashed Ivan while Keith was staggering out of the Bull & Rhubarb one Wednesday night. Jason McKenzie and I watched from behind a bin while Ivan waddled over and called Keith the 'Karate Kid' (because he used to karate kick me back in the day) then delivered a few of his signature fake punches to Keith Morris's turkey neck. Even though we knew they were fake, Jason McKenzie and I fell for those punches every single time. It genuinely looked like he was going to punch Keith and we would gasp with each retracted fist. Old Conspiracy Keith (don't worry, that nickname didn't go unused) kept asking who Ivan was and flinching at every fake punch before attempting to run away into the night. He lost a flip-flop in the process which got swiftly stolen by a street dog. Ivan, Jason McKenzie and I held a debrief in a secluded area, sitting on top of a skip round the back of a fish and chip shop (I would later compose a poem about the evening in which I rhymed 'chip shop' with 'flip-flop' but kept it to myself because I got embarrassed). Straight out the gate, Ivan expressed how grateful he was for his new writing team.

'Before I met you guys, I used to improvise my verbal bullying on the spot and I just sounded dumb. I'm good at fake punches and my size is intimidating but I could tell my words never cut through. But this material you wordsmiths are giving me? Stellar. I feel like I'm the total package now. I got the muscle, the attitude and the gift of the gab – I could bully anybody!'

I'd never seen Ivan be this enthusiastic. We'd made a young man believe in himself and it felt good to inspire the next generation.

The greatest bullies in the world

The following day we made a list of other potential grown-ups for Ivan to bully. This is where Jason McKenzie's old job as a primary school teacher really came in handy. He'd taught so many bullies over the years and most of them were adults now, making them prime candidates to be bullied by their ex-teacher and his pen pal via a primary school kid. Coming up with material for Ivan was a rewarding but demanding task. He wanted specific insults for each target, not the same old, one size fits all, recycled hack name-calling that any bozo could come up with. Writing for Ivan was especially stressful because he was a literal bully and if he was unhappy with our work then we'd receive a fair few fake punches for our trouble (which we fell for every time) and a barrage of offensive language (poorly written because it was his own gear). But such things were a rare occurrence as, all in all, the bullying went off without a hitch. We bullied a man called Ralph Barely by calling him Ralphy Bare-Bum and making him cry in front of his place of work (TK Maxx), we bullied a lady by the name of Vikki Skarsgaard by calling her Lady Guffington (because she was posh and once passed wind in a PE lesson when she was seven), and we bullied John and Yvonne Ammersley for being twins. For a few weeks, we were nailing it, we turned bullying into an art form. Jason McKenzie and I felt like Magritte, and Ivan was our Frankie Boyle. The world was our oyster, we could bully it as we pleased and eat all its pearls . . . but we got too cocky.

One night, when getting ready to bully Tiffany Mandelson (another of McKenzie's ex-pupils, used to gob in her classmates' pencil cases), we presented Ivan with a gift bundle, something to show he was part of the gang – a membership card to The Rebuttlers Fan Club, an official Little Joey's sippy cup, some fake sideburns just like the ones Jason McKenzie and I wore, and the latest edition of the *Tangfastic Echo* with him as the cover story ('Punching Up – How Ivan Martin Is Changing the Face of Bullying'). The message was simple. We were all one and the same, we were a team – a team of great bullies.

Unfortunately, the fake sideburns combined with his build made Ivan look like an adult man and Tiffany Mandelson chased him five laps round a dog-walking park while trying to hit him. As he ran, Ivan breathlessly tried several times to say, 'Please, I'm a child,' before we grown-ups clambered down from our safe place (up a sycamore tree) and explained ourselves. The explanation saved Ivan but ultimately resulted in Jason

McKenzie and me getting beaten up by Tiffany Mandelson. I'd like to tell you that Ivan didn't switch sides and join in with the beating but that would be a lie. The kid's a natural born bully. His instincts kicked in and he wanted in on the action. He and Tiffany made quite a formidable team and gave us a proper hiding. Once it was over Ivan gave us our sideburns back and said thanks for the memories but that he was joining forces with Tiffany now. We then had to lie on the grass in pain and watch while the two of them choreographed a new handshake for their dynamic duo. It involved a lot of fake handshakes reminiscent of Ivan's fake punching, which sounds tacky but honestly, it gave the whole routine a personal touch most handshakes lack – nice work all round. I made a mental note to come up with a Tangfastic Crew handshake and maybe even a password. Make that two passwords, actually – one for the castle and one for the crèche.* I know it sounds odd, but as we twitched in the grass, Jason McKenzie and I couldn't help feeling proud of our protégé. It's not like we could blame Ivan for betraying us – Tiffany had been a bully since the age of five and had a lot of wisdom to dispense in that arena. Jason McKenzie and I were mere rookies who hid behind bins and let children get their hands dirty on our behalf. We called out and told him we understood, he should follow his bullying dreams and do what makes him happy. Then he stamped on our hands and ran off into the night.

---

* Many weeks later, I'd settle on 'moat' for the castle and 'kids' for the crèche.

All's right with the world

Jason McKenzie and I are still working at the school, of course. A week after Ivan double-crossed us, we bumped into Callum Michaels (AKA Cal-bum My-balls) on his bicycle and asked him if normal service had resumed.

'Yeah, the respite was nice while it lasted but Ivan's bullying me again,' sighed Callum, now sans his top hat. 'I'll tell you what though – his insults have got much better. He calls me Ball-scum Bike-Bells now!' Then he rang his little bike bell and giggled with glee.

This news warmed our hearts. I guess we'd made a difference after all. We told Callum we were glad to hear it and that if he wanted any comebacks writing then we had plenty of time to spare (we still weren't doing the actual janitorial work, even with Ofsted looming).

Sometimes we pass Ivan in the disease-ridden corridors, his heavy footsteps reverberating off the ceiling like church bells on a Sunday morn. He rarely acknowledges us but on occasion he does wear the Tangfastic T-shirt and, if we're lucky, we might even catch him whispering the crew's official password as he trundles by ('tangfastic'). The other day we threw a fully inflated basketball at his head for old time's sake, then after school we got ambushed by Tiffany Mandelson and she kicked our heads in.

On the subject of throwing basketballs at kids' heads, we did give this approach one final go but added a little twist. I'd recently remembered the time I'd filled a bunch of water balloons with honey and thrown them at children on their way to school. Jason McKenzie suggested we combine the two ideas and fill a basketball with honey before launching it. A great idea on paper but it just made the basketball extremely heavy, like a medicine ball, and we still count ourselves lucky that we missed that particular kid's head. The honeyed basketball was confiscated by Headmaster Brown who promptly took it down to the zoo and threw it in the bear enclosure so it didn't go to waste. I'm told this was a big hit with the bears who were able to play with the ball as well as drink from it and the zoo have since made 'honeyball' a regular part of their timetable, proving once again that there is no such thing as a bad idea even if that idea is throwing a basketball loaded with honey at an infant's head.

How do I Embarrass My Kids Now?

Hanging out at a primary school had given Jason McKenzie and me a taste for picking on minors and reminded us of yet another online-ism we were regrettably missing out on – trolling kids within your own family.

Social media has been a game changer when it comes to parents humiliating their children. Being able to embarrass their offspring with horrendously uncool status updates and pathetic tweets that do as much damage to their own reputations as they do their kids' has given parents a much needed edge in the battle of young versus old. With the click of a trackpad, they can destroy the life they once created and then claim they had no idea this would even be an issue. A mother can comment, 'You go girl!' on a photo of their daughter leading a business seminar. A dad can misjudge banter with his son's friends and look like an unfunny pillock. A parent can post numerous photographs of themselves looking bald as hell and yet inexplicably refuse to wear a hat every time they have their photograph taken. In short, there's never been a better time to be a cringeworthy parent than now. I myself have no kids to speak of (when you run a crèche, having kids is a bit of a busman's holiday) so when I left the old socials I lost nothing when it came to embarrassing my non-existent offspring. My good friend and business partner, Jason McKenzie, on the other hand, had a real-life son named Howard.

Howard McKenzie

Howard McKenzie is fourteen, he likes heavy metal music and lives with his mother. From what I gather, he hates Jason McKenzie and has zero interest in ever seeing him – awful for Jason but, on the plus side, it made embarrassing Howard the easiest thing on the planet. If there's one thing I know it's this: it is extremely difficult to embarrass a kid who likes you. In an ideal world, you want your kids to find your very existence objectionable. Once you've achieved this, you can humiliate them simply by being alive. Naturally, this became our first plan of action – to find out where Howard McKenzie was and just be there. But this proved trickier than we first thought.

We hit up all the places we'd hang out if we were modern-day teenagers – art galleries, libraries, garden centres etc. – but they were full of cool grown-ups rather than the modern youth. We tried asking people where the teenage hot spots were but either nobody knew or nobody wanted to tell us. I never appreciated how easy the internet had made it for adults to locate kids until I needed to find a group of kids without the internet's help. Online, grown-ups are able to run wild, talking to every single kid in the whole wide world and everyone lets them get on with it. People treat you with so much suspicion if you want to hang out with teenagers in the real world, especially if you're two grown men dressed in backwards baseball caps, tie-dye T-shirts, baggy camouflage bottoms and roller skates.

Our thinking behind the outfits was that kids find it especially humiliating when their parents try to be cool. I would've loved to have seen the look on Howard McKenzie's face if we'd rocked up to his friendship group saying, 'Hey, hey, what's crack-a-lacking, daddio?' while wearing our tie-dye garb. But we never got to see that priceless expression because strangers kept threatening to call the cops on us whenever we asked where the kids were at. I think a lot of people mistook our outfits for 'disguises' and assumed we were trying to trick the kids into believing we were also kids. As much as we resented the accusation, it did remind us that catfishing existed online and this caused us to get a little sidetracked. Jason McKenzie and I would never EVER catfish a minor – I cannot be clear enough about that – but both agreed that catfishing adults had always looked like a laugh. My time spent as Jaym Baecaster had been a blast, spoiled only by me losing my entire sense of self. Jason McKenzie was fairly certain that if we catfished people in the real world instead of online, it'd be much easier to maintain a grip on our true identities, especially if we did it together and one could pull the other out if they were going too deep. This conversation escalated (to put it mildly) and led to us spending a month of our lives as Christopher Jam and Dallas Hemsworth.

Jam & Hemsworth Ltd

Christopher Jam and Dallas Hemsworth were two oil tycoons looking to drill a little black gold in Muswell Hill. Straight out the gate, I was determined to make them the most convincing characters we'd ever played. I wanted to improve upon the disguises I'd worn when spying on Penelope Crouch so we splashed out big-style on professional, movie-quality facial prosthetics, perfected our Texan accents and constructed two believable backstories. This was by far the deepest Clancy Dellahue had ever delved into her wallet but, luckily for us, it was also the idea she thought sounded the most fun so was happy to part with the cash.

Christopher Jam (me) had grown up on a ranch and made his first million when he accidentally struck oil burying the family's house pet, a goat by the name of 'Scruggly Tom Scruggins'. Since then, he's been married seven times and exec produced a short-lived quiz show on the Brainbox Network called *Wha' Dat?*; it was cancelled after six episodes due to being a blatant rip-off of British quiz show *Catchphrase*.

Dallas Hemsworth (Jason McKenzie) was born in Louisville, Kentucky, on the banks of a swamp and spent his summers taming 'gators by playing The Mamas and the Papas' back catalogue on a plastic kazoo. He founded the tech company Opti-Vision in 1993, out of which came Infra-red Contact Lenses, Foggles (goggles that could see through fog) and Impossible Spex. Impossible Spex was the invention that made him his fortune.

'I remember hearing everyone saying they needed eyes in the back of their head so I combined the humble glasses with the humble periscope, introduced the humble slinky and hey presto – I had me a pair a Impossible Spex.'

It really is amazing how quickly one can take to being a liar. As soon as we had our disguises on, Jason McKenzie and I found lying to people's faces to be as natural as breathing (even though breathing was quite difficult under several layers of prosthetics). We went speed dating in character and told lady after lady that we were going to make a shit ton of money once we'd freed the sweet oil from beneath Muswell Hill. We got a full house of matches but only chose to see Katherine and June again, as they seemed the easiest to catfish. Within a week they had both accepted our hands in marriage. Our proposals were terribly romantic. Jason McKenzie and I took our dates to the top of the London Eye (we told them it was owned by Opti-Vision) and when that big old wheel reached the top, we both got down on one knee and asked them to marry us in unison. We then threw in a little bonus lie and announced that Dallas Hemsworth had decided to convert each of the pods on the Eye into one-room apartments and would be selling them to first-time buyers, adding that the Eye would still rotate at the same rate, giving each resident a stunning view of London for five minutes every hour. It was an unnecessary fib to lob in the mix but our brides-to-be thought it was genius, cementing their decision to take our hands in holy matrimony even more. After the ladies went home to tell their friends the good news, Jason McKenzie and I agreed that this was a good place to end the experiment so we threw our costumes in the bin and returned to our normal lives.

Finding Howard

Once we'd said goodbye to Jam and Hemsworth, Jason McKenzie and I promptly remembered we were supposed to be humiliating his teenage son, Howard McKenzie. We'd fallen way behind on this project due to playing oil tycoons and catfishing two nice women to their faces. However, we'd emerged from that experience a wilier pair of individuals and were certain Howard wouldn't elude us a second time. We may not have known any of the cool teenage hangout spots but we absolutely knew for a fact where stupid Howard would be every weekday from 08:30 to 15:10 – that's right, a little place called 'school'. And guess what – that's where all his dumb friends would be too. Howard would be a sitting duck, quacking in front of all his duck pals, wide open for a couple of wily geese to waddle over and make him look silly by trying to pass themselves off as cool ducks for no reason. We both agreed humiliating Howard at school was the way to go, all Jason McKenzie had to do was quickly ask his ex-wife what Howard's school was called and we were all set.

Jason McKenzie's ex-wife was incredulous that he didn't already know the name of his own son's school and launched into a lengthy but totally justified rant about parenting and how Jason McKenzie was the worst at it. Luckily, during said rant, she did mention the name of the school as well as Howard's age, middle name and birthday, so we left mid-rant and applied for jobs as janitors at Howard McKenzie's secondary school.

Janitors again

Jason McKenzie and I already had janitorial experience thanks to working at the primary school where we bullied kids and taught kids to be bullies, so becoming janitors at a secondary school felt like the next logical step. Getting the job was easy, *doing* the job was the hard part. Straight out the gate, we were warned by the head of the custodial staff that teenagers make five times as much mess as the average primary schooler because they're old enough to realise that being messy is cool. They're forever littering and pushing stuff over because their street cred goes through the roof every time they act like they don't care. How right he was. We may have been the bullies back in primary school but we were about to become the *bullied* in big school. These kids were knowingly making our job a waking nightmare and they didn't give a solitary toss what that did to our precious little feelings. That being said, this teenage obsession with appearing cool could clearly work in our favour. It's almost impossible to embarrass a primary school kid because they don't care about looking cool, they just want to run around scoffing sweets and talk extensively about Lego. Teenagers, on the other hand, are a piece of cake to embarrass because being cool is their entire life. Naturally, Jason McKenzie and I have zero respect for people who spend all their time trying to be cool, it's an incredibly sad way to live and we have no qualms whatsoever in toppling the tiny worlds of such people especially if their name is Howard Anakin McKenzie.

The zeitgeist

Having said that, one thing we'd been extremely worried about since quitting social media was becoming uncool. There was a very real danger we'd drop out of the zeitgeist and we simply couldn't have that. If we dropped out of the zeitgeist then we would cease to be cool and being cool meant a lot to us because it was our entire life.

Finding ourselves in a secondary school five days a working week meant we could eavesdrop on teenagers like nobody's business (and it literally was nobody's business) and make notes as they discussed all things 'geist: poorly made TV shows, horrendous celebrities, pathetic dance crazes and what parts of the human body were now considered ugly. Jason McKenzie and I made note of the latest political hot takes (Joe Biden looking old, voting being pointless) and stayed on top of any new turns of phrase ('mega-thrumpt', 'them broomsmen are bare creepy', 'jiggle that iggle 'til it ain't got no piggle'). We may not have understood half of what was being said but we walked around regurgitating it non-stop (we later learned that 'broomsmen' meant janitors) and, as long as we dodged any follow-up questions, everyone assumed we were well and truly on top of The Big Z (the large zeitgeist).

More than anything else in this book, I would say keeping on top of The Big Z is essential. If you don't work in a school then you're going to have to start sitting near kids on buses or getting a booth next to them in McDonald's. If you're not plugged into the zeitgeist, then you may as well be dead. Good luck and remember – keep it thrumpt.

Humiliating Howard

Before I get back to how we embarrassed Howard McKenzie, it's also worth noting what my life was like at this stage of my offline story. I was running my own crèche, working in both a primary and a secondary school, attending university and hanging around a lot of celebrity funerals. Every single day was a cradle-to-the-grave experience for James Acaster. I have never appreciated the full gamut of life and all it has to offer as much as when I came off social media. Every single day I lived an entire lifetime – like a mayfly. And, just like a mayfly, I never once looked at social media while I was doing it. Ever wondered why you never see a mayfly on Facebook? Because mayflies understand the time we have on this Earth is precious. That's why they spend their twenty-four hours of life doing the two coolest things imaginable – having sex and flying.

Juggling two janitorial jobs was a little much at times. Running back and forth between the two schools was exhausting but the exercise did us good and if we were out of breath when talking to Howard McKenzie's friends, well, that'd just embarrass him even more. Seriously though, we were *so* embarrassing. Howard McKenzie loooooves standing around with his goth mates, just outside the school gates, smoking super-cool-dude cigarettes and talking in an unenthusiastic tone about stuff he dislikes. Enter Jason McKenzie and his younger friend, James Acaster, dressed in lavender overalls (custom-made especially to embarrass Howard), walking in a way we thought looked cool but was actually stupid (lifting our knees too high and stepping too far out to the sides) and greeting the group with the phrase 'toodle-oo' even though it technically meant goodbye. We always made sure we were talking loudly for no reason and used Howard's name in as many sentences as possible (I'd estimate that 100% of our sentences included the word 'Howard'). We would try and be rad by pointing at a cigarette one of Howard's friends was smoking and saying, 'Can I hit that, Howard's friend?' then we'd hold it very delicately between our thumb and forefinger, the rest of our fingers fanned out like we were doing the hand signal for 'A-OK', and take cautious little puffs before exhaling and nodding like we thought it was 'good shit'. Howard hated this. We would also make announcements about our own lives that nobody asked for. Jason McKenzie would give loud updates on the arts and crafts company he'd started from home, letting all of Howard's friends know that he'd just finished prepping a batch of Silly Straws. That's straws with googly eyes attached to the bendy bit so it looks like the straw has a face and is some sort of creature in its own right. Jason McKenzie informed Howard's pals that they would be available for purchase from Pancake Day onwards. I invited the group to our pancake day bonfire, where we would always be making up to 50 pancakes at any one time. I also loved to interrupt Howard by asking his friends what they were up to over the weekend, not listening to them and making announcements about my own life. You should've seen Howard McKenzie's face when I promoted the welly wanging semi-final the Scouts were hosting that coming Tuesday. Teenage goths love to pretend that they don't know what welly wanging is. As if they were never anything but goths and didn't wang a welly as kid. Jason McKenzie and I could see right through them so we would often push welly wanging as a topic until we caught one of them out. Once caught out, the teenager would be forced to admit they had indeed wanged a welly at one stage in their lives. One kid, Ignacio, flat-out refused to confess to ever welly wanging. At first, we called bullshit but when we cornered his parents at home time and asked them straight up if Ignacio was playing us, they confirmed their son had never participated in any wanging of any description, let alone the welly variety. So we let him be. After all, we wanted to embarrass these kids by using who they *really* were against them and the Lavender Boys weren't in the business of making stuff up.

Oh yeah, Jason McKenzie and I started referring to ourselves as the Lavender Boys. We came up with the name because we exclusively wore lavender to school and would declare ourselves the Lavender Boys every time we saw Howard and his pals by calling out, 'Toodle-oo, it's the Lavender Boys.'

The Lavender Boys

Operation Embarrass Howard was off to a flying start but we still felt like we could do better so we began interrupting his lessons. Naturally, we claimed that we needed to clean his classroom, but once we were in the door, we did zero cleaning whatsoever. We would deliberately fall over, talk to each other loudly about running a crèche out of Jason McKenzie's bachelor pad and occasionally we'd raise our hands to answer the teacher's questions. It should be noted that most teachers welcomed our questions as it was nice for them to receive a little enthusiasm for a change. They'd point at us and say, 'Yes, the Lavender Boys,' and most of the time we'd just tell them they were doing a great job. Howard's classmates absolutely loved us. They thought we were daft and good for a laugh. Howard's close friends certainly found us entertaining if a little eccentric. Howard himself spent most of his school day wishing he could jump into a live volcano. That's not a phrase I've plucked out of nowhere, he said it out loud on multiple occasions: 'I wish I could jump face-first into a live volcano right now.' Howard McKenzie said the volcano thing so often that the whole class began joining in every time he screamed it into his trenchcoat. It was funny.

Things couldn't have been going better but Jason McKenzie and I had forgotten the one risk that came with embarrassing teenagers in front of their mates – sooner or later, the mates will decide you're a legend and end up preferring you to Howard McKenzie. It wasn't long before the goths had swapped their black robes for lavender garments and were wanging wellies from noon to night. Jason McKenzie and I did not see this coming and, while we were delighted to welcome some new blood into the Lavender Boys, we felt bad that Howard was now left to smoke roll-ups on his own while peering through his dyed black fringe at the accidental cult his father and I had created. Luckily for us, Howard solved all of our problems by doing the mature thing and moving schools. It was a huge weight off our mind. The Lavender Boys could now continue to thrive while Howard McKenzie started a new life God knows where (his mother wouldn't let Jason know the name of Howard's new school so your guess is as good as mine, but we'd wager it's one with a high goth count). I'm happy to report that The Children of the Lavender Sun (Lavender Boys was pretty sexist so we switched it up and decided to lean into the obvious culty vibes) went from strength to strength and before long we had Howard's entire school year dressed head to toe in lavender. Inevitably, we folded The Children of the Lavender Sun into the Tangfastic Crew. The Tangfastic Crew had already been a little culty, after all, so what harm could a little extra cultiness do?

I can feel some of you judging us because 'cults are bad' but I saw this as a massive win. We're constantly told the lie that social media will bring us together and we feverishly buy into that lie while those very same sites push us further apart and make us feel isolated from the rest of humanity. But here I was, cut loose from the binds of all socials, and within a year I'd become the leader of a sizable cult. What brought all these people together wasn't the internet, it was each other. And me. Well, mainly it was me. I brought everyone together. But I wouldn't have been able to bring everyone together had I remained online. Once The Children of the Lavender Sun had all painted over their phone screens with tar and made the necessary journey to Rhyll, the Tangfastic Crew were sixty-three members strong and we could finally begin to take on some bigger, more ambitious projects.

GIFs and Memes

Oh baby, nothing makes the dreary days zip by like a well-timed GIF or an appropriate meme (or an inappropriate meme, am I riiiiiight?!?!!) and as my post-internet life continued to blossom, I did experience a little GIF-drawal. I needed to get my MeF fix. Yes, MeF is a mash up of a meme and a GIF – I'm a MeF addict, so sue me. It was time to conjure up some real-life substitutes for GIFs and Memes, a little MeFodrone, if you will, and this led to the Tangfastic Crew's biggest triumph yet. But I'm getting ahead of myself. Before I landed on the perfect solution, I had to kiss a few frogs. Here's how NOT to do things . . .

GIF fail

For my GIF substitute, I initially tried going to the cinema and walking out after the first five seconds of the movie. Sounds perfect but it wasn't the same. It's amazing how a GIF can convey so much in just one brief moment and these so-called 'feature-length films' barely get into their own credits given the same amount of time. If every Hollywood blockbuster ended after the first five seconds, they'd all be shit and if every GIF went on for two hours, they'd be the best film you've ever seen. Better than *The Godfather*, *Citizen Kane* and *Austin Powers* combined.

Even so-called 'short films' feel too long when compared to GIFs. Short films should be called long films, if you ask me. What's impressive about short films is not only are they boring when compared to a GIF, they're also boring when compared to a feature film. Surely the one thing a short film has on its side is that it lasts fifteen minutes rather than two hours and yet, somehow, that fifteen minutes always feels like the slog of a lifetime. They're usually set in one room, they feature virtually no special FX and the characters either won't shut up or don't talk at all. Every short film is either silent or crammed with more words than a boring book. Before you say it, yes, I know that most GIFs are set in one location and feature no dialogue but they make up for it with a little thing called action – a word no short-film director has in their vocabulary! I once saw a short film where the high point was someone sliding a coaster under a glass. They clearly wanted me to go away and think about it but I refused to. The last thing I want to do is make a short film last even longer by thinking about it afterwards. For years people assumed short films were boring because they didn't have enough time to get the audience fully invested in their story the way a feature film does. Then GIFs came along and blew that theory out of the water and up a duck's ass. The fact that the short film category at the Oscars is yet to feature a single GIF nomination is criminal. John Travolta once mispronounced Idina Menzel's name at the Academy Awards, called her Adele Dazeem and the GIF of him doing that has currently been watched more than any Best Picture winner in the last hundred years. That should tell the Oscars something. To be clear: I'm not implying that John Travolta saying 'Adele Dazeem' should've won Best Short Film at the Oscars. Of course not. It was an unscripted slice of real life and therefore should've won Best Documentary Short. It would have slaughtered the competition too because the only thing more boring than a short film is a short documentary. Docs are always trying to teach you something and, newsflash, learning is boring. The only thing the Travolta GIF teaches us is how not to say Idina Menzel – a valuable lesson that I'm more than happy to take on board. Beyond that, it's pure, uncut entertainment featuring a Hollywood A-Lister at the top of his game. And it didn't even get longlisted. Anyway, I'd drawn a blank as far as GIF substitutes were concerned so I gracefully pivoted into the wonderful world of memes.

Meme fail

For my meme substitute, I turned my gaze to the caption competition in my local newspaper (the one Daniel and I delivered). The winning caption each week was as close to a meme as real life got. I'd laugh at those captions until my lungs were raw and my throat was hoarse. One week the picture in question was of nineties footballer Steve Bruce shaking hands with someone dressed as a pepperoni pizza and Niall Presley from Ormskirk had submitted the caption 'Nice to meet you, to meet you, Slice'. Even though he'd mixed up his Bruces, it still made me howl and I think about it on a bi-weekly basis. The winners of the caption competition were exceptional and I relished the way their minds worked

BUT meming isn't about winners and losers. Meming is about community. It's about everybody throwing their ideas into the pot and passing round the stew. I wrote to the newspaper asking if they would consider publishing every submission they received instead of just the winner but they wrote back saying they get asked this all the time and definitely can't be bothered. They also said they'd heard about the *Tangfastic Echo*, absolutely didn't appreciate us launching our own rival paper and vowed to crush us if it was the last thing they did. What followed was some rather ugly correspondence. I'd rather not share those letters with you because, full disclosure, I come across appallingly in them.

Besides, handwritten letters are the real-world equivalent of a DM – they're between the writer and the sender and should stay that way. Unless, of course, one of them chooses to make the letters public in order to destroy the other – then they're between everyone on the planet.

I'll say this for *The Daily News*: even though we were locked in a war of words, exchanging vile letter after vile letter (sometimes a vile postcard if one of us was abroad), they kept their feedback regarding my caption competition entries entirely separate. The main problem I had with the caption competition was that *The Daily News* clearly weren't familiar with memes and the tropes that come with them. One week, they presented their readers with an image of a man riding a penny-farthing through a carwash. I turned this into the perfect meme, submitting the caption 'TRYING TO ERASE THE SINS OF MY PAST LIKE' and received a lengthy letter asking not only if I was OK but why I had ended the caption with the word 'LIKE'. I mention the penny-farthing in a carwash because it illustrates another problem I had with these caption competitions – nine times out of ten, the image they provided was already funny. An angry lady carrying a box of boomerangs, a child in a business suit consuming a massive jelly – we can all agree these images are good value but there's nothing you can add. I'm already laughing at a kid in a business suit on sight, I don't have time to hear your pithy one-liner on the issue (even if 'Sales are a little wobbly today' did make me snort Tizer out my nose. Kudos, Gordon from Thrapston).

The more I thought about it, the less caption competitions functioned effectively as meme substitutes. Memes are a highly sophisticated art form and a pathetic contest run by a bunch of gaslighting hacks wasn't going to satisfy my needs. It slowly became clear what I'd need to do in order to get my MeF fix – I'd have to cook up some of my own. I'd have to make my own GIFs and my own memes from scratch. There was no other way. What follows remains, by far, the most expensive project Clancy Dellahue has ever reluctantly funded.

The creative process

First of all, I had to write the GIF scripts. This was a painstaking process and involved plenty of rewriting but eventually I'd scribed some solid gold screenplays I knew were going to knock people's socks off. Here are some of the finished GIF scripts for you to feast your eyes on but, before you do, little tip – hold on to your socks (see previous sentence for why).

BATTER UP

by

James Acaster

EXT. BASEBALL STADIUM - DAYTIME
SHOWN IN DOUBLE SPEED:
It's the day of the big game and
ALPHONSO is up to bat, only he is
holding a battered sausage instead of
a baseball bat. The pitcher throws
him a doozie but ALPHONSO swings
and misses. He is declared out and
throws the battered sausage at the
floor in frustration, only to have it
rebound off the plate and hit him in
the shin. He hops around in pain.
REPEAT THE ABOVE FOREVER.

BABY ON BELT

by

James Acaster

INT. SUPERMARKET - MORNING
URI is working at the checkout. He
scans items as they arrive along
the conveyor belt. A box of cereal.
A frozen chicken. Then, to his surprise, a live human baby!! URI does
a big double take. The baby looks
up at him while sucking a dummy.
REPEAT THE ABOVE FOREVER.

LAKE

by

James Acaster & Jason McKenzie

EXT. LAKE - EARLY EVENING

A man falls in the lake.

REPEAT THE ABOVE FOREVER.

SCARED

by

James Acaster & Jason McKenzie

INT. CIRCUS - DAYTIME

A juggler is chased by a baby ele-
phant.

REPEAT THE ABOVE FOREVER.

CURSED

by

James Acaster & Jason McKenzie

EXT. SNOW-COVERED FIELD - AFTERNOON

A snowman comes to life and does a
dance.

REPEAT THE ABOVE FOREVER.

```
                WHAT GOES DOWN
                MUST COME UP
                      by
         James Acaster & Jason McKenzie

INT. FIRE STATION - NIGHT
A fireman slides down the pole then
slides back up again.
REPEAT THE ABOVE FOREVER.



                PRESIDENT DRAGON
                      by
         James Acaster & Jason McKenzie

EXT. RALLY - MORNING
A politician opens his mouth and
fire comes out of his mouth.
REPEAT THE ABOVE FOREVER.



                      FART
                      by
         James Acaster & Jason McKenzie

EXT. MONASTERY - MORNING
A monk farts.
REPEAT THE ABOVE FOREVER.
```

And there's plenty more where that came from.

Lights, camera, action!

The great thing about filming GIFs is that, while you need the same size crew and equipment as a feature, the GIF itself only takes a matter of seconds to film. With that in mind, I decided to hire a full film crew with all their equipment for the same amount of time it would take to make a feature-length motion picture (four months) and used that time to make five thousand, two hundred and eighteen GIFs. There were two crews on set, the film crew and, of course, the Tangfastic Crew. Offline Hors D'oeuvres provided the catering, Little Joey's Crèche looked after any child actors, Daniel drove the cast to and from their trailers in Old Chitty and Dr Hetty was our on-site first aider (despite not being that kind of doctor). The Children of the Lavender Sun stepped in as runners, location scouts, set designers, camera operators and the entire wardrobe department. The Rebuttlers made up the production's legal team and a man named Roger Deakins was our director of photography. Next, I needed a fine cast of actors to bring my GIFs to life and I was adamant I wasn't going to cheat by getting the same people to play multiple characters throughout the series. This meant we had thirteen thousand, four hundred and fifty-nine roles to cast, not including background actors. I already knew I was going to play one of the roles. I had my eye on the lead in a GIF entitled 'HEAVEN'. 'HEAVEN' was a real GIF for the ages: an angel (me) eats their bodyweight in marshmallows then gets a high five from Jesus. I could see the public using the 'HEAVEN' GIF in countless situations, namely ones where people feel like they're in heaven and want to illustrate it by using a GIF that sums up how brilliant being in heaven is. Casting Jesus was difficult. Technically it was just a supporting role but culturally it's a big deal and comes with a lot of baggage attached to it. I wanted to be historically accurate so we made sure we cast an actor who was literally born in Bethlehem and grew up knocking about Jerusalem. We saw over two hundred 33-year-old hopefuls but eventually we went with a guy named Abdel, a superb actor who could deliver a terrific high five without even looking at the person he's high-fiving. Most films give us some Westernised abomination of the Messiah and they certainly never make him fun – they just focus on him getting beaten up or fully killed. Our Jesus was geographically legit and, instead of getting wailed on by some dickhead Roman, he was loving every second in heaven with his friends. Abdel was a total professional, he researched the character heavily, reading any material he could find (mainly the Bible) and nailed the high five in one take. Off camera, Dr Hetty loved getting Abdel dressed up as Jesus and bringing him along to her midnight confessions. Father Douglas absolutely hated Abdel and asked Dr Hetty on numerous occasions not to bring him but she wouldn't listen. 'When you've got a guy who plays Jesus better than anyone has ever played Jesus, you're going to invite him to confession, honey.' Abdel wanted to serve as a reminder to Father Douglas that the chain of command goes higher than the priesthood and he would often hammer this home by trashing the old priest's church. Abdel's favourite Bible story was when Jesus trashes the Temple and he loved recreating it at every opportunity, regardless of the context. Needless to say, Abdel is a firm member of the Tangfastic Crew these days and we couldn't get him out of his Jesus costume if we tried (which we never would because having a friend who permanently looks like Jesus is badass).

Actors

We cast a lot of actors in a lot of GIFs, a mixture of new faces and big-name stars. I won't bore you with the new faces because they're nobodies but the bona fide stars we got on board included the likes of Sally Field, Alyson Hannigan, Djimon Hounsou, Will Ferrell, J. K. Simmons, Monique, Anna Farris, Eugene Levy, Bill Murray playing a talking prawn and Daniel Day-Lewis. And I'm pleased to report – not a diva among them! Apart from Daniel Day-Lewis, who was a nightmare. Daniel Day (as we call him in the biz, although I often just called him Day for short) remained in character the whole time he was on set. He was playing Jeffrey Dahmer in the GIF 'Helpful Dahmer' in which a serial killer assists an old lady across the road. I received numerous complaints about Day throughout filming from crew and co-stars alike because he scared the shit out of everyone. Filming the GIF itself may have only taken five seconds but it took hours to set up and dismantle the shot either side of it, and during that time Lil' Danny Day Louie ran amok like you wouldn't believe. He terrorised every single member of the crew by jumping out on them and ferociously growling, 'I'm Dahmer,' through his bare and gritted teeth (which he hadn't cleaned in months). He did it to me on more than one occasion and I did not appreciate it. I tried to tell him off once but he ran away cackling to himself and then bit a boy. It was stressful to say the least but when all's said and done, I can't argue with the end product. Day didn't just play Dahmer, he *was* Dahmer and I think you can sense that when watching the GIF. When filming wrapped, Day declared that 'Helpful Dahmer' would be his farewell to acting. Obviously, we've all heard that song and dance before but this time I'm confident he means it. Mainly because he's now serving life in prison for murdering seventeen people during filming and isn't likely to be released as he's a danger to society. Pretty grim stuff. I only ask that you don't let this sully your enjoyment of the GIF and please separate the artist from the art.

Distribution and retail

Incidentally, if you would like to own one of my GIFs on DVD, you can. We printed LOADS of copies and I regularly try and flog them at markets up and down the country. So far, I've managed to flog one DVD and one DVD only, to a lady in Hartlepool who originally visited the market looking for trinkets. The poor woman was struggling to find the right sort of ornament for her mantel and this reminded me of a GIF I'd made where a man places the Venus de Milo on a shelf in his study causing the entire thing to collapse on him, his arms ironically (and comically) being severed amid the hubbub. Once I'd described it to her in detail, she purchased 'Venus de My Shelves' and sped back to Hartlepool to watch it forever. She wrote to me a week later, thanking me for giving her the gift of the GIF and remarked on what a lovely surprise it was to see Nigel Havers in the leading role. I know it sounds corny but if I can change just one life with my filmmaking then I'm basically better than a doctor. I feel like I've achieved that with 'Venus de My Shelves' and the life I've changed is that of Nigel Havers. His career was on the rocks before we revived it. You're welcome, Nige.

Memes can come true

If you can make your own GIFs, making your own memes is a piece of cake. I hired a whole new batch of expensive sets and another raft of famous celebrities (John Turturro, Sandra Oh, the farmer from *Babe*) to populate the world of our memes. I already owned a lovely camera and had my work featured in countless exhibitions all over the country so it made sense that I would handle my own meme-ography. I took fifty photos in the end. I know that doesn't seem like much when compared to the amount of GIFs we filmed but you must remember that memes are recycled constantly – the image stays the same but the captions are ever-changing. So yes, I only took fifty photos but each of those photos gave birth to a thousand memes. For example:

> **IMAGE:** Bradley Whitford raising one eyebrow at a donut while a dog steals a second donut in the background.
>
> **MEME 1:** Bradley Whitford. A donut. A dog. (Always start by labelling the image literally or people get confused. Now you can have a little fun with it.)
>
> **MEME 2:** Democrats. My vote. The Illuminati.
>
> **MEME 3:** God. Humans. Partying hard.
>
> **MEME 4:** Me. My dream job. Rich kids.
>
> **MEME 5:** Jason McKenzie. Jason McKenzie's ex-wife. Jason McKenzie's friend Burt Brosnan.

Jason McKenzie hates that last one but I think it's funny. I've not shown it to Jason McKenzie's ex-wife or Burt Brosnan but

I think they'd see the hilarious side. From what I gather they're very happy together and both used to be a laugh when Jason McKenzie hung out with them so I'm sure they'd get a kick out of a little meme humour.

The award for the hardest meme we ever had to shoot goes to the image of Moira Stuart ziplining over a swimming pool full of electric eels. The final product looked breathtaking. The waves bursting and flashing with blue light like a million light bulbs cranked up to the max, Moira looks like an action star as she soars above the ferocious glow, a little kid stands on a diving board like he's making his mind up whether to jump in or not. So much being said in just one image. But, crikey Moses, it took an age to capture. Stuart kept refusing to do it because she'd assumed we wouldn't be using real live eels. We kept telling her they weren't dangerous but that was a hard sell as the eels kept zapping both me and the diving-board kid. I'd say, between us, the kid and I got zapped sixty-one times. The kid took the lion's share of those as he was naturally curious and kept leaning over the edge of the pool to get a peek, receiving a zapping every time. Despite the fuss, Moira Stuart got zapped zero times, even though she completely fell into the pool at one point. It was the first photo we took, she lost her nerve halfway along the zipline and sploshed into the water but none of the eels gave her any grief. The eel handler said the eels were probably 'zapped out' from me and the kid. Once she knew that, Moira Stuart zipped down that line with grace and panache and it was a joy to see. The kid's parents have since written to me, expressing their concerns that their child blatantly still has electricity in him. His dad described his son as being 'chock full of watts'. Apparently he's able to turn on appliances with his touch and occasionally zaps his enemies for his own pleasure. I sent the eel handler (the same guy I'd bought Enid from) to pay the family a visit, hoping he could talk some sense into the kid but, just like those eels, the kid didn't respect the eel handler's authority in the slightest. The eel handler phoned me afterwards and said, 'That kid was more like an electric eel than any human being I've ever met.' He may have added, 'May God help us all,' I can't remember. Obviously shaken up by the encounter, the eel handler then flapped his gums to every journalist in town and it became front-page news. I consoled myself with the fact that this was yet another news story I had known about before it got anywhere near social media, even if the only reason I knew about it was because it concerned me getting a kid repeatedly zapped by a pool full of electric eels. It became national news before long and the ironic day came when Moira Stuart had to report on her own news story. I'm told that the image of Moira Stuart reporting on her own meme with the meme itself in the top right corner of the screen has become a whole new meme in its own right and won Meme of the Year at the Annual Meme Awards. So, yeah, you could say my memes have been a success.

I know that on paper it reads like making my own GIFs and memes cost a pretty penny and, yes, the costs did feel astronomical at the time but the amount of joy I've accrued day after day from the very same GIFs and memes – you can't put a price on that (but also you can and it's $250m). If you still don't understand the appeal, then I guess the only way I can truly describe how these homemade GIFs and memes make me feel is this:

HEAVEN 2

by

James Acaster & Jason McKenzie

INT. ICE CREAM PARLOUR - DAYTIME

A man downs a giant tub of chocolate ice cream. JESUS jumps into frame and he and the man chest bump.

REPEAT THE ABOVE FOREVER.

Viralness

Back when I was an OI (Online Imbecile) I was able to throw together a meme, post it on social media and watch it spread like luxurious marmalade across the poisoned, mouldy toast of the internet. Now I was offline, my network was smaller and I could only share my memes with my Crew or look at them solo. In short, I was essentially eating an entire jar of marmalade all to myself while offering the occasional teaspoonful to a mate, and even though eating an entire jar of marmalade was a delicious thing to do, it didn't feel 100% healthy. I couldn't lie to myself any longer – I wanted to go viral. I needed the validation that only comes with millions of people liking something you've done, sharing it with each other and consuming it like golden, crispy marmalade churned from the teats of the juiciest oranges in all of MarmaLand.

'String Theory'

After much consideration, the Tangfastic Crew agreed that 'String Theory' was my best meme and therefore the most likely to go viral. The image was that of a cheesestring taking its driving theory test at the DVLA with the caption 'ME UNDER

PRESSURE' in bold across the bottom. We loved it because we'd resisted the urge to write 'STRING THEORY' as the caption and instead made the meme about how we all feel like giant pieces of melting string cheese when put under pressure. The only people who knew the meme was even called 'String Theory' were its creators. This is the case with all memes. The creators know the true title of the meme but never disclose it to the public once it's out in the world, leaving it open to interpretation. Every meme has an official title – 'Winner Baby', 'Creepy Kid Arson', 'Man Staring at a Woman's Butt While His Girlfriend Looks Appalled' – and this one was called 'String Theory'. Clancy Dellahue managed to get a million copies of 'String Theory' printed on A1 card. You read that right – one million copies – we're going viral here not running for valedictorian. With the cards printed, Daniel and I took a stack each, hopped on our bicycles and got 'ready for a spready'.

The two of us were already experts at hand delivery because we were papermen and knew how to hop on our saddles and fling literature at the unsuspecting public. We soon discovered that a rigid A1 piece of card flies a little differently to a rolled-up newspaper and encountered our fair share of close calls (translation – Daniel nearly took a gardener's head off) but for the most part we managed to frisbee our precious memes into people's homes with ease (it helped if they had a window open or, at the very least, that long thin window at the top of the main window open).

Nice little story: during our meme delivery, Daniel and I had a discussion about the term 'viral' and how much nicer it would be if instead of referring to the spreading of a nasty disease it referred to the spreading of something pleasant like marmalade (I've actually worked elements of this conversation into this very chapter. Go back and see if you can spot them!) During this little chat, Daniel said, 'If a meme went viral, people could spread it like MEME-alade,' and if you don't find that funny, you should reread it or read it out loud this time because, guess what, it is funny – simple as. Also around this time, Daniel invented a cocktail called a meme-a-colada. He basically went through a stage of coming up with meme puns. A meme-a-colada is a pina colada but you look at a meme when drinking it. And yes, we do sing the famous song while we're making them: 'If you like meme-a-coladas and getting caught in the meme.'

Celebrate good memes, come on

Once we'd delivered one million memes, it was time to celebrate going viral. I booked the soft play area Pandemonium for the evening and Offline Hors D'Oeuvres would be providing the catering.

Jason McKenzie began serving up sliders and spring rolls while the rest of us slid, sprang and rolled all over Pandemonium's squidgy interior. However, for Daniel and me, something didn't quite feel right. Going viral, technically, is when a million people share your brilliant meme of their own free will. Whereas we had just sent a brilliant meme to a million people without their consent.

Oh no.

We hadn't gone viral – we'd spammed a million people. We immediately panicked, trying to convince each other everything would be OK. Maybe the recipients of the spam would share the spam of their own free will, spreading it like pâté throughout the neighbourhood (we changed the metaphor from marmalade to pâté. It only felt right to opt for a meat-based spread going forward). But we knew the dream was over. We articulated our fears with the crew and it was agreed that what we had achieved here was a spamming and not a viral. Jason McKenzie immediately cursed the heavens.

'I nearly put Spam on the menu, as well! We could've pivoted seamlessly into a spam party!'

'We still can,' Bernice the wonder baby piped up. Bernice reminded us that the main thing I was trying to prove by deleting my social media was that it's possible to live an online life offline. So every time I achieved an online thing out in the real world, it counted as a victory. This meant I could chalk up another win for Project Offline because Daniel and I had just become a couple of massive spammers. I declared the party back on and the Tangfastic Crew celebrated until they could celebrate no more AKA until Dr Hetty chipped her tooth on a padded roller and threw a strop AKA the party lasted another twelve minutes.

Tangfastic virality

We all put our heads together and realised that going viral didn't necessarily mean spreading something *physical* far and wide. Going viral could also consist of everybody *talking* about something you'd created, preferably with excitement, and telling all their mates about it. And then it hit us. We had this awesome organisation that most people didn't know existed – the Tangfastic Crew. If we could let just a few people know how rad the crew was then maybe those people would tell their friends and maybe *those* people would tell *their* friends and, before you know it – hey presto – we've spread across the world like golden meme-alade (we switched back to marmalade once we'd ditched the whole spamming thing).

We swiftly set about spreading the gospel of the Tangfastics. We whispered in people's ears about this awesome crew that runs a crèche, a catering company, has a debating team and holds vigils for dead celebrities. We even printed off a few flyers and got my team of targeted flyerers to distribute them far and wide. When it came to selling ourselves, we focussed on our USPs: the entire group was offline, we had zero internet presence and were all about doing things 'the old-fashioned way'. We had our own newspaper, our own T-shirts and our own mode of transport in the form of Old Chitty. Some of us were adults and some of us were teenage children (one was a primary school child if you include Ivan the Bully but he comes and goes as he pleases). Heck, we even had a baby as a member if you include Bernice, although she's still too busy working on her thesis to admit she's a member of the crew. To which I would say, 'Stop turning up at our soft play parties then, Bernice! You had seven Spam tacos last time!'

The flyers we'd printed out all included the address of our HQ (the good Castle Anti-Net) – our thinking being, we'd only know if we'd gone viral once people got in touch with us and asked to join up. If we reached a million crew members, we'd know word had sufficiently spread and we'd achieved our viral goal. And so, after all the flyer distribution and all the whispering in people's ears, plus the expensive billboard campaign that Clancy Dellahue sorted, we sat back and we waited.

Spoiler alert – we went viral, mate.

Verified

You heard me right. The Tangfastic Crew now consists of three hundred and seventy-five people!! I know we said that we had to get to a million in order to go viral but once you see three hundred and seventy-five people all packed into one soft play area, you realise what viral really is. It took us just shy of five weeks to get there but, honestly, those five weeks flew by and felt like no time at all. One morning we were in double figures the next we were in triple figures – even a calculator couldn't argue with those numbers. We were multiplying like rabbits but, unlike rabbits, we'd done so while keeping it in our pants (we all agreed that babies we'd made ourselves didn't count as new members when going viral).

The new crew members took to being Tangfastic like ducks to water (or like ducks to land. Ducks can thrive on both). Each of them painted over their phones with tar and threw them in storage, before choosing a division to work in. With this many hands on deck, everything ran a lot smoother. My TV reviews rocketed in quality because I now had a proofreader and, even more importantly, a ghostwriter on board – freeing me up to focus on leading the Tangfastic Crew and conducting catfishing operations. We were catfishing new people every single day. Those of us who acted in GIFs were able to keep the costume, stay in character, walk off set and casually catfish someone without missing a beat. A lot of the catfishings started generating a lot of dosh too. We had many, many projects that needed funding so if some lonely widower wanted to transfer us a wad of cash because he thought he'd fallen in love with the heir to the throne of Siberia (who needed help settling a debt with her father's rivals) then fine. We get a little cheddar and some widower gets to hear a funny little story about the Siberian royal family – everyone wins.

What I had on my hands here was incredible. I wasn't just able to make friends offline, I was able to make business associates, I was able to launch an entire organisation. Back when I joined Facebook for the first time, I had also joined a little site known as LinkedIn. It's a more professional, business-y form of social media, where someone can network and grow their business, maybe even get a job, who's to say. Certainly not me, seeing as I never once looked at that site after joining it. In fact, LinkedIn was the only social media profile I hadn't deleted when I left. Not because I couldn't bear to part with it but because I had literally forgotten it even existed. One day, while marvelling at my own ingenuity, counting the amount of independent businesses I'd knocked out of the park, I realised that I'd done it all without the business face of the internet – LinkedIn. Nowadays, it's viewed as impossible to get a business off the ground without being on LinkedIn. People won't take you seriously unless you're on that site! The first thing any business mogul asks in an important business meeting is, 'Are you on LinkedIn?' and if the answer is no then you may as well go home right now and flush your briefcase down the toilet. Oh, how the people of LinkedIn would turn green if they knew about me – the man who launched a newspaper, a crèche and a cult without even owning a computer! The LinkedIn empire would surely crumble if word got out. Their trillions of users would start to ask questions LinkedIn would rather go unanswered. Questions like, 'Excuse me, LinkedIn. You've launched the careers of Steve Jobs, Richard Branson and Duncan Bannatyne but has this little businessman named James Acaster proved there is another way?' There was no denying it. I was "LinkedIn" all right – linked in to people and their hearts.

Businessmen need business cards, so I sauntered over to my local printing company and had them print me up a buttload.

JAMES ACASTER –
FOUNDER AND CEO OF THE TANGFASTIC CREW.

JAMES ACASTER –
LEAD REBUTTLER. EVERY DISQUALIFICATION COUNTS AS A WIN.

JAMES ACASTER –
LEAD TV CRITIC AT SING HOSANNA!

LITTLE JOEY –
LITTLE JOEY'S CRÈCHE

And on and on and on. Card after card after card. Proper professional-looking. Gold letters embossed on a cream background. It'd taken a lot of blood, sweat and tears but I was finally official. I was certified. I was *verified*. These business cards were the real-world equivalent of a blue tick. I actually had them print a blue tick in the top right-hand corner of each card so everyone would know I was verified now. It looked the bollocks too. Now I was verified, people would respect me, they'd take me seriously, they'd be unable to use my name instead of their own name in public forums. James Acaster – Verified Human Being. I liked the sound of that.

Naturally, I got a buttload more business cards printed saying 'JAMES ACASTER – VERIFIED HUMAN BEING' on them. I forgot to include the blue tick on those ones though, so the general sentiment got undermined somewhat. But we live and learn. Hakuna matata etc.

Bottom line – I'd done it. I was a verified boss in charge of a 300+ strong organisation who knew how to get shit done while staying off the grid. It occurred to me one day, while watching some Tangfastic members remove their wigs and snowshoes after a long day's catfishing, that we could make a real difference now we had a crew of this size. We could start to achieve things no one ever thought we could've pulled off without phones or social media accounts. It was time to shake things up good and proper. It was time to make a statement. It was time to dish out a little justice. It was time to go out into the world and get people fired from their jobs. It was time to have people thrown in prison. It was time to do a little real-world cancelling.

Tangfastics Assemble.

Let's Get Cancelling

I'd never got to cancel anyone back in my online days but the people who did always made it look like a hoot. Sure, I might've been a little green but I didn't mind learning on the job and couldn't wait to cancel some scuzzy piece-a-crap off the face of the Earth. First, the Crew needed to settle on a target, preferably a celeb. After much to-ing and fro-ing we all agreed that Babs Brillington fitted the bill perfectly. You may know Babs Brillington as Radio DJ Sensation Tam Brillington's widow, but we knew her as a scuzzy piece-a-crap. She had been rude to us when we were in mourning and refused to acknowledge our grief. The man we were mourning was her dead husband, Tam Brillington, and she berated us on the day of his funeral ('Move your vigil, you inconsiderate swines, be gone!') – a day she surely knew would mean a lot to us as we processed our emotions and grappled with the treacherous beast that is loss.

After doing some digging, we discovered Babs had cheated on Tam back when he was on the Breezy FM Roadshow in the late nineties (Tam was a standby DJ and also driving the bus). Daniel had gained access to her medical records and noticed that she'd had an STI test during the months while Tam was away and you don't have to be a doctor to figure out what that means. The next morning, we popped over to her place of work, a lovely local opticians, to inform her of the cancelling, only to find her absent. The chief optician, a man by the name of Marky Gillespie, informed us that he had, in fact, recently fired Babs. Initially, we began to celebrate what had already been a successful cancelling, until we learnt why Babs had lost her job. We had assumed it was due to her past infidelities but it turned out Marky Gillespie was quite the bigot and, after years of biting her tongue, Babs had finally stood up to his hate speech only to be given the sack. He had given her the old heave-ho the previous day and she was already down at the courthouse pursuing legal action against him. The crew asked Marky Gillespie to excuse us and formed a huddle near the spinny glasses stand – when we emerged, we told him he was cancelled.

Marky Gillespie is cancelled

We greeted Babs as she, two of her friends, her mum and her lawyer exited the courthouse. At first, she was extremely hesitant to interact with us but Daniel and I assured her everything was fine and that we were totally over the death of her husband.

'We want in,' we told her. 'We want to bring down Marky Gillespie.'

Babs appreciated our support and began reeling off a bunch of ways in which we could help. None of which we listened to because we already knew the lay of the land and, the next day, we pulled Marky Gillespie's pants down. We got him in the park and everyone saw his penis. We ran away yelling 'Justice for Babs' over the laughter of the masses and filmed the whole thing on my camcorder (we screened it a month later in a cinema as a short film before the main feature, which in this case was Biffy Clyro live at The Hydro). Babs found us later that day and told us off, saying that our behaviour was damaging her case or some baloney. She really wagged the finger and when she left, we were all rather perturbed and felt unappreciated.

'Who the hell was that?' asked Kelvin Rodgers and I told him not to sweat it. Kelvin Rogers had joined the cause in the park after seeing how pathetic Marky Gillespie's penis looked. We had recruited around twenty-five new crew members that afternoon and our numbers were growing by the day (unlike Marky Gillespie's nob!). Every time we served Marky Gillespie his just desserts we'd get bystanders wanting in on the action. We gained 52 new members after pulling his pants down in Waitrose, 394 new members after pulling his pants down at the Emirates, a few thousand new members after pulling his pants down on the local news and one new member after pulling his pants down in front of the postman. We were killing it! Meanwhile, Babs and her 'legal team' were failing to get anything to stick to Marky Gillespie because they couldn't prove any of the stuff he said and he refused to admit to any of it. To make matters worse, there were a whole bunch of people on Marky Gillespie's side – other bigots, mainly – who kept throwing eggs at Babs's house and sticking notes to her back that said 'Kick me'.* Granted, most of my crew didn't know about any of that, they were mainly into pulling people's pants down and laughing at them, but for Babs it was devastating. For ages she kept on asking us to stop pulling Marky Gillespie's

---

* Can't remember the last time I saw someone stick a 'Kick Me' note on someone's back. These guys were old school through-and-through.

pants down as it was detracting from the true message and causing more people to egg her house blah blah blah blah but eventually, after months of being let down by the legal system, Babs phoned us up – she wanted to talk.

The following weekend, Babs pulled Marky Gillespie's pants down. Because it was the only thing left for her to do. And we all had a good laugh at his penis.

Cancelled

We cancelled many people in this fashion and we got pretty damn good at it. The Crew was now in its thousands and we could de-pants someone any time, any place. Sure, a lot of people criticised us, questioning our methods and suggesting that exposing people's genitals was unhelpful. But they were missing the point. If the justice system actually worked then we wouldn't have to pull down so many people's pants – we could cancel people by taking them to court and successfully chucking them in the clink. The way we saw it – if the Marky Gillespies of the world got to walk free then their genitalia should walk free also. Even the people whose pants we pulled down never actually got fired or sent to prison, they just pulled their pants back up and carried on doing whatever they wanted. It was a weird time.

We'd been cancelling steadily for a few months when we got Vernon Reems in our sights. At first, Reems seemed like any other scuzzy piece-a-crap ripe for cancelling. His newspaper, *The Daily News,* had been involved in a phone-hacking scandal. Turns out, they'd listened to one of the Mayor's WhatsApp voicenotes to his head of PR, a recording of him singing a potential jingle for his next campaign. They used this to launch a story all about the Mayor being tone-deaf (musically and politically) and made fun of him for rhyming 'constituency' with 'I'm bitching, y'see'. The consensus of the general public was that *The Daily News* were bang out of order for the phone hacking so the Tangfastic Crew de-pantsed Reems while he was queueing at the post office (yes, we yelled, 'Special delivery!'). But there was one small detail I was forgetting. *The Daily News* had dirt on me. Hundreds of handwritten letters from yours truly threatening to do all sorts of unspeakable stuff to them if they didn't a) admit that the *Tangfastic Echo* was the coolest paper in the world or b) let me win the caption competition. The day after we pantsed Reems, *The Daily News* printed every letter I'd ever sent them in the latest edition of their stupid newspaper. A double-page spread. Threats to throw every reporter they had into the Grand Canyon. Threats to slap them silly (a quote I'd heard in *Home Alone*). Threats to shove various objects up their rectums, usually objects that were bigger than the average rectum and would therefore hurt if shoved up there. Staring at my own handwritten aggression, laid out in black and white, sent shivers through my entire being. I thought I was gonna be sick. Everyone would think I was a bad person. I'd be persona non grata. Sure, *The Daily News* had also been considerate enough to include my caption competition submissions, so my meme work was gaining some exposure, but that didn't quite make up for the volume of hate I feared would be coming my way. Little did I know, things were about to get far worse than I'd ever imagined.

Once *The Daily News* had printed the letters, other snitches started coming out of the woodwork. Father Douglas, the unprofessional swine, told everybody I'd been deliberately bullying people. He described in great detail the time I threw a fully inflated basketball at a child's head and bullied him for it after. Not once did he mention Jason McKenzie's involvement in all this – just me. He made me sound like a monster. Worse still, word soon got out that I myself had been hacking people's phones for ages, something I'd totally forgotten about until I saw it in the newspapers. Ex-girlfriends, celebrities, celebrity agents, I'd hacked way more phones than *The Daily News* and then I'd 'had the nerve to pull their pants down when they did it'. All my chickens were coming home to roost and now I was drowning in feathers, beaks and chicken plop. I had to watch my back everywhere I went and never left the castle without wearing two belts and some industrial strength braces in case anyone tried to de-pants me for my sins. Worse than that, the Tangfastic Crew began acting weird around me. Crew members were avoiding eye contact, dodging conversation, even the OG members like Demetri and Jason McKenzie were uneasy in my presence.

One afternoon, I ventured out into the world, wearing a boiler suit so no one could pull my trousers down, and I wasn't handed a single flyer by my own targeted flyering team. Even the people I'd paid to approach me didn't want to draw near! I turned up at the crèche but was halted at the front door by a swarm of parents. They'd decided they were no longer comfortable with me being Little Joey and had handed the title over to Kiki Gosling. I looked over at the living room window to see Kiki singing 'Wind the Bobbin Up' with the babies and glaring at me from behind the painted glass, her face framed by a demented elf sliding belly-first down a rainbow. This became a running theme for the rest of my day. I was turned away from my university (apparently some of the questions

I'd asked in my Cultural Studies class were 'concerning, to put it mildly'), The Rebuttlers replaced me with some guy called 'Disagree Lee', both my janitorial jobs told me to get lost, even my paper round was handed over to Ivan of all people – the biggest bully of them all! Sure, he was more age appropriate when it came to being a paperboy but he'd bullied way more people than I ever had. Case in point – he immediately bullied my trusty bicycle, James Bike-Faster, off me for his paper round (with Tiffany Mandelson's help, as per).

As I trudged back to Castle Anti-Net, a shell of my former self, the heavens opened and it began to rain. I got drenched. I don't know if you've ever worn a wet boiler suit but they're heavy as hell and it took me twice as long to get home because my defeated bones were too weak to lift my own thousand-ton outfit. By the time I reached the castle, I was sodden and could barely even lift my head, but when I eventually did raise my eyes to my safe abode I quickly wished I hadn't. The drawbridge was raised. A sight I'd never seen upon arrival. Usually my crew would spot me on the approach and lower the drawbridge for me, playing a cassette of fanfare samples as I made my way inside. But now, for the first time in my life, I was staring at the unwelcoming visage of a closed castle, the rain dancing off the moat, too wide for me to leap over and too deep for me to wade through. I instantly regretted ever buying a spade. I tried yelling for my crew to let me in but I could barely hear my own voice above the distant thunder and the roar of the torrential rainfall. I briefly caught a glimpse of Isaac peering at me through one of the arrow slots but he disappeared swiftly. So it was like that, was it? I was officially cancelled by my own crew. As if to cement this fact, some local kids darted out of the bushes and de-pantsed me before running off again. Obviously, when you're wearing a boiler suit, a de-pantsing is way more drastic than usual as it involves stripping the mark (in this case, me) of their top also. They somehow tore the whole thing off and ran away with it into the storm. I was left wearing my official Tangfastic boxer-briefs and heavy-duty janitorial boots, sheets of rain lashing my pale body as I screamed up at the punishing sky, a man alone.

A man alone

The days that followed were some of the hardest I've ever known. I was banned from Castle Anti-Net and kicked out of the Tangfastic Crew. They'd dumped my business cards into the moat where Enid zapped them all to ash. I was no longer verified, I was no longer anything. I was a nobody. I tried, on numerous occasions, to regain entry to the castle but for nought. I must say, I got pretty good at pole-vaulting in a surprisingly short space of time. I never made it inside but I'd perch on a ledge and press my ear to the stone in an attempt to listen in on any conversations the crew were having, especially ones about me. I was worried they may have forgotten me, that now I was out of the crew they might not talk of me any more. Truth of the matter was, they talked about me a lot and that was worse. I ended up hearing a lot of stuff I didn't want to hear. They'd slag me off noon 'til night and every time a comment particularly hurt my feelings I'd lose my balance, tumble from the ledge and get zapped in the moat by Enid. I felt like a loser. Why was I doing this to myself? Why was I relentlessly putting my mind and body through such heartbreak? Why had I not sourced some clothes yet? The underpants and boots were holding up fine but I looked mad and was permanently freezing.

One evening, as I dragged my freshly zapped body out of the moat, my face was met by an unfamiliar pair of shoes but a very familiar pair of legs. The shoes could've been anyone's but that shade of denim could only belong to one person. I looked up, moat water dripping from my fringe, to see the stubbled face of Tom Space smiling down at me. He offered me his hand.

'Need some help . . . Friend?'

Return to Space

I emerged from the bathroom in my new outfit and Tom applauded.

'You look great!' he cheered.

The white T-shirt and blue jeans fitted perfectly and made a comforting change to being soaked to my skin in the cold outdoors. Tom's condo had seen better days but I was grateful he'd taken me in. I had no idea he'd been living so close to the castle this whole time.

'I've always been here for you, JPeg. Whenever you needed me.'

I nodded because I'd always known it was true. Dane Cook was making cocoa in the kitchen while the Arctic Monkeys slept in a pile in the corner of the living room.

'We all moved in together not long after you left the 'Space,' explained Tom. 'I just wanted to make sure the crew stayed tight, y'know?'

And I did know. I knew all too well. I heard the sound of the front door opening and the shuffling of someone taking off their shoes and jacket in the corridor. Tom looked at me, dewy eyed with a sentimental smile.

'Sounds like someone would very much like to meet you, buddy.'

I turned around to see a middle-aged man standing in the doorway. His plaid sleeves rolled up to the elbows, steak sauce on his cheeks and chin, beads of sweat dotted across his brow, he was grinning in a way that was both welcoming and off-putting.

'Hello Ernie,' I said.

Ernie Freedman gave me a warm bearhug as if we were old chums.

'Welcome to the Tomdo!' he boomed. 'It's like a condo but Tom owns it. Get it? Tom-do!'

Yep, he was a dick but he was treating me better than anyone else was right now. I gave 'Tomdo' a fake laugh and sat down to drink cocoa with Tom, Dane Cook and, of all people, Ernie Freedman. I never dreamt I'd meet Ernie Freedman in real life, let alone have a civil conversation with him over a freshly made warm mug of cocoa. He seemed blissfully unaware of any animosity I'd ever harboured towards him and instead reminisced with me about the good old days on MySpace. He spoke like we were MySpace friends back in the day, I don't think he even remembered rejecting my friend request. I suppose to him it hadn't been that big of a deal. Now that I'd met Ernie Freedman in the flesh, I couldn't possibly take anything the big galoot had ever done personally. He was essentially an affable fella with his big dumb head in the clouds. Blessed with a lack of self-awareness that meant he'd never read into life's tinier details and interpret them negatively, he'd only see what was on the surface and give it two hollow-skulled thumbs ups. Ernie was all right. It was me who'd been out of order. I'd had it all: my best friend Tom, Dane Cook's comedy, the music of the Arctic Monkeys and Ernie Freedman, the reliable pal I never knew I had. But I left them. I left them to pursue a life that didn't exist. I thought that if I came offline then I could reclaim control of my life and no one could hurt me any more. I was wrong. As a bleary-eyed Alex Turner led the room in an acoustic rendition of 'You've Got a Friend in Me' (from the *Toy Story* soundtrack), I knew that these were my people and I needed to reconnect with them ASAP.

Return to Rhyll

As the train to Rhyll pierced the Welsh countryside, I felt good. The plan was simple – I'd go to Fill 'Em Up Rhyll 'Em Up, retrieve my devices from storage, smash the tar off the screens and rejoin the online community once and for all. I'd tried living my life offline but it'd only got me right back where I started – naked and alone while being zapped by an electric eel. I couldn't wait to be bathed in my laptop's warm glow once more, to feel the weight of my phone in my palm, to lay my eyes on the MySpace logo and know that I was truly back where I belonged. Real life had been too much, too visceral, like coming round from anaesthetic mid-operation and seeing everything exposed and bloody for the first time, the realisation that you're living in a horror film and everything could end at any time. I'd tried it and it wasn't for me. I wanted to switch off again, I wanted to go back to Facebook, back to Twitter, back to Instagram, where everything felt real but deep down I knew it wasn't. I wanted to hide.

Stepping off the train at Rhyll Station felt like the first chapter in my new life. The sun was shining and the birds were singing. Normally this'd be a nice thing but I was done with the real world. I was ready to put shining suns and singing birds behind me and dive headfirst into a life full of sun and bird emojis instead. As I strode though the town with my head held high, I was already fantasising about the conversations I would have online. How good it would feel to be *retweeted* again! The closest I'd come to a retweet in real life was when Jason McKenzie would steal a joke I'd made in conversation and pass it off as his own later on. Online it felt great to get a retweet but in real life I always felt like Jason McKenzie was ripping me off and giving me none of the credit. I couldn't wait to relaunch all my old profiles and receive a hero's online welcome. Everyone would go berserk, telling me how much they'd missed me, liking every status I posted just to let me know how loved I was. It was going to be incredi—

'Hey, Acaster! Come back to die on your arse again, you shit comedian prick?!'

I stopped in my tracks. A mum and her kids were grinning at me from their doorway. Judging by the timbre of the voice it'd been the mum who shouted at me.

'Pardon?' I half-whimpered.

'She said,' yelled the local milkman as he drove past on his milk float, 'your comedy is shit and we all remember that gig you did here and how shit you were!'

Oh God. I had to get to the storage facility pronto.

I sprinted through the godforsaken streets of Rhyll as stranger after stranger yelled abuse at me because I'd sucked when supporting Milton Jones on tour in 2011. A florist threw a plant pot full of soil (no flower) at me and a vicar genuinely sounded gutted when it failed to hit me in the head. I slammed the front doors of Fill 'Em Up Rhyll 'Em Up behind me, panting as I tried to catch my breath. I'd forgotten how much this town hated me. I'd stopped visiting long ago and allowed any new Crew members to make the pilgrimage by themselves. The jeers of the Rhyllanites were yet another reminder of how cruel the real world could be. I made my way through the labyrinth of storage units, recovering from my latest ordeal, trying to focus my mind on happier times to come. I'd soon be back online where everyone was kind to one another and the general public left me alone. I froze in front of the door to the Tangfastic storage unit. My eyes fixed on the combination lock. My breathing slowed as I reflected on that last thought.

Where everyone was kind to one another and the general public left me alone.

Bullshit.

Bullshit

I knew it was bullshit and couldn't keep on lying to myself. The abuse I was receiving out in the streets of Rhyll may have been brutal but online, everyone could hunt me down whenever they felt like it and remind me of every shit gig I'd ever had – and I'd had LOADS. I slowly turned the numbers round in the combination lock, 2-0-0-3, the year I'd joined MySpace. As the door swung open, thousands of phones and laptops spilt out of the unit like an electrical landslide. I was waist high in tar-covered dormant devices, no clue whatsoever which ones were mine and which belonged to another crew member. I waded into the unit itself, my eyes adjusting to the dark as I rummaged around fruitlessly. My heart suddenly didn't feel 100% on board with this plan. I didn't want to go back online but equally, I wasn't that up for leaving here empty-handed with the residents of Rhyll chanting 'shit comedian' at me. As the first person to deposit their device in this storage container, I knew my phone and laptop would likely be right at the bottom of this technological bog. I took a deep breath, filling my lungs with tar-tainted oxygen, and dived beneath the surface. I burrowed like a sad gerbil into the murky depths, groping blindly for my precious old friends, bashing my head, face and elbows on the corners of laptops and, at one point, nearly choking on a flip-phone. The big breath I'd taken lasted fuck-all time and it wasn't long before I was huffing tar underneath a pile of PCs and Macs. I felt woozy, everything began to soften at the edges and my head spun like a Lazy Susan at a carnival workers' tea party. Amid the darkness I caught a glimpse of a glimmering white light. I swam towards it with ease and, before I knew it, found myself washed up on the shores of a desert island. The sand was fine and bright pink, the island couldn't have been bigger than a traffic roundabout, a blue-trunked palm tree in its centre with bright orange leaves, bowing towards me as if in greeting. As I clambered to my feet, I could make out the form of another, resting against the base of the palm tree, with their back to me. As I made my way round to identify them, I was met by a most familiar face. My own. Well, more or less my own. This character certainly resembled me but was dressed entirely in black and cream with a ten-gallon hat atop their dozing bonce.

'Jaym Baecaster, I presume,' I spluttered, as Jaym's eyes slowly opened, blinking in the sunlight. I looked around, the brilliant green waves stretching for miles.

'Where are we?' I asked.

'We're where you've always been trying to get to,' Jaym replied. 'On a weird island where no one can hurt us.' He rose to his feet, producing a bowl of pasta out of thin air and proceeding to eat as he spoke. 'I used to devote so much time and energy to arguing with people about whether Crowded House were good or not that I forgot to simply enjoy the sublime tunes of Crowded House. I was so focussed on letting people know I loved climbing walls that I never found the time to do any actual climbing.' He slurped a particularly long strand of linguine past his pursed lips and continued. 'You created so much for yourself out in the real world but never got to enjoy any of it because you were so preoccupied with getting others involved. You didn't feel enough without their validation and now here you are, trapped underneath a pile of plastic and tar, hallucinating that your old Twitter alias has come to life. Heck, you only invented me because you were too concerned about what others would think of you returning to social media!' he said, emptying the last of the bowl into his pasta-loving mush.

'You're right,' I said, dazed. 'It was never the internet . . . it wasn't even the real world . . . it was . . . it was . . .'

Suddenly Jaym and I were face to face, his eyelashes touching mine. He placed his hands on my chest and smiled in a way that told me to trust him.

'It was us,' he said and pushed me into the sea.

I gasped for air as my body rose out of the tarry detritus. Two Rhyll 'Em Up employees dragged an arm each until I was lying on top of the mountain.

'Bloody hell, lad,' the older of the two exclaimed, 'you can't go diving into piles of mobile phones like that, people will think you're mad!' I looked down at my hands to see one was gripping a laptop, the other a phone. Upon closer inspection, they were *my* phone and *my* laptop. I'd rather not speculate as to how this happened, it was just magical and that's the important thing. I sat up to look at them and immediately started sinking again. The Rhyll 'Em Up employees dragged me out and called me a tosser. I stood up in the corridor, examining my long-lost devices. They didn't feel as familiar as I'd anticipated. I think I'd expected a more emotional reunion, a few tears minimum, but I kind of felt nothing. I let them fall from my hands and they clattered back into the pile, merging with the rest of the crap until I couldn't pick them out any more.

'Shall we get all this back in storage now or what?' said one of the employees and I smiled.

'What,' I answered proudly.

How I live now

It took only a short time to empty all the tar-covered devices out into the corridor but once they were out, the storage unit itself looked very inviting. I changed the combination lock to 1-9-9-2, the year I started writing to Jason McKenzie, then I stepped inside, closed the door and listened as the confused employees locked me in.

The employees here aren't paid to ask questions. They've been very accommodating. As long as I pay for everything, they'll do my weekly shop for me. They sourced me a mattress and duvet and even supply me with a bucket of hot soapy water each morning for wash time. I never see them but I think that's the way they'd prefer it. They've made no bones about how weird they think the whole thing is but I don't care. I like it here.

Looking back, I think I actually enjoyed the lockdowns of 2020 and '21. Those months when I'd stayed indoors and focussed on a personal project had been the happiest of my entire life. No internet access and limited human interaction while achieving actual life goals – and now I'd found my way back to that. I wrote this entire book from within my storage unit – the magical pencil the enchanted old man gave me came with a luminescent eraser tip that lights the entire room like a desk lamp. I'm going to tell the employees to drop my manuscript on the doorstep of the first publisher they can find. I have no idea if any of this will even see the light of day. I'll never know. I'll just chill out in here, satisfied that I even wrote it and that'll be enough. Although I really hope I don't get any bad reviews.

Every now and then, I'll hear a new member of the Tangfastic Crew arrive at the storage facility to chuck their devices into their new unit. It's next door to mine and I'm often awakened by the shifting of phones as they open it up. One afternoon, the newbie was accompanied by Jason McKenzie. I knew it was him because I recognised his voice as he sang the Tangfastic Anthem in his usual sombre tone. For the first time, I was tempted to reach out beyond these four walls and talk to someone – to my best friend. Yes, we'd fallen out but I still felt tethered to him somehow. Maybe if I extended an olive branch, he'd open up his arms to me and everything would be OK. Alas, I didn't have the strength to do so. I'd been burnt too many times and couldn't put myself out there again. Those days were over. As I sat in the dark, listening to the clanging of unit doors and the clickety-clacking of combination locks, I had to accept that in order to be happy we have to make sacrifices and accept what we've lost. If being alone was the only way I could avoid having my feelings hurt, then so be it. I exhaled deeply. Everything fell silent. And then the door opened.